The
Hypochondriac's
Handbook

A DISEASE FOR EVERY OCCASION

AN ILLNESS FOR EVERY SYMPTOM

JOHN NAISH

Harper
Collins

FOR HEALTHY KATE

HarperCollins*Publishers*
77–85 Fulham Palace Road,
Hammersmith, London W6 8JB

The HarperCollins website address is:
www.harpercollins.co.uk

First published by HarperCollins*Publishers* 2004

4

© John Naish 2004

John Naish asserts the moral right to be
identified as the author of this work

A catalogue record of this book is
available from the British Library

ISBN 0 00 719568 0

Printed and bound in Great Britain by
Clays Ltd, St Ives plc

CONTENTS

INTRODUCTION

Let's invent a new illness. Let's call it Modern Hypochondria Syndrome. The symptoms? Gnawing health anxiety; fascination for new diseases; an impulse to throw cash at costly therapies; excessive use of words such as 'well-being' and 'nutrient'. Risk factors: living in a comfortably rich nation and having a lack of real threats to fret about. We've just created MHS, a new and worrying social disease. Easy.

Well, it was no harder than inventing Pleasure Deficiency Syndrome, which a survey of 2,000 people has warned is sweeping Britain. In November 2003 the survey, by the pollsters YouGov, quoted the psychologist Dr Linda Papadopoulos claiming that PDS victims suffer tiredness, boredom with work and lethargy. 'There is evidence that people are malfunctioning because they are not enjoying enough pleasure on a regular basis to be healthy happy people,' she says.

If that doesn't get you throwing your arms about in panic, then consider Celebrity Worship Syndrome, which apparently affects one in three Britons and is 'borderline pathological' in severe cases. CWS victims can be 'impulsive, troublesome and insensitive', says the *Daily Mail*'s report on 14 April 2003 of a study in the *Journal of Nervous and Mental Disease*. So watch out, or one day you might wake up to find yourself stalking a daytime-TV gameshow presenter.

CWS is hardly the Fifth Horseman, is it? War, Plague, Famine, Death and Celebrity Worship Syndrome. But such silly sicknesses are becoming epidemic. The developed world is safer than ever, but new 'illnesses' continually emerge to keep doctors, therapists and drug companies hale and hearty. Our appetite for the latest threat seems insatiable.

We all, to some extent, carry the germs of hypochondria. We evolved mild doses of it as a survival tool. Our cavepersons' brains are hard-wired to obsess about threats. We relish tales of strange and deadly illness like winter-nights' horror stories. Thanks to modern sanitation and medicine, those dangers are now no longer anywhere near so real. But at the same time, civilization has given us much more time, cash and energy to spend fixating on sickness. So the Western world has enjoyed a huge drop in mortal illnesses – and witnessed a leap in new diagnoses.

How many people (psychopaths apart) do you know who, deep down, are cheerfully convinced that there is absolutely nothing wrong with them? I bet that if you were to put on a pair of white overalls, drive an ambulance-type vehicle along the high street, pull up next to any pedestrian, leap out and say, 'Get in, we've found out what's wrong with you', most would willingly be helped limply into the back. Go on, try it.

Many doctors worry about the trend to prescribe ever more new drugs and treatments for an ever-growing list of new illnesses. The British Medical Journal in April 2002 polled British doctors on the top 'non-diseases' that are being redefined as medical conditions. In first place was ageing, followed by work, boredom and bags under the eyes. Others included baldness, freckles, ugliness, jetlag, shortness, nail biting, bad breath, insomnia and hairiness.

But many other doctors are keen to discover, or invent, new illnesses for us. It gets them published in the profession's fast-expanding body of story-hungry research journals. If their new disease is scary enough – or sexy enough – it might get their name in the newspapers. And if they can specialize in treating their new illness it could make them a lot of money.

The old demon money lurks behind much hypochondria. The pharmaceutical industry needs new plagues as badly as the rest of us. If it cured everything, commercial growth would grind to a shareholder-sickening halt. The industry thrives by providing cures – though companies have found it is a cute trick to invent cures for diseases that don't quite exist. They, after all, are much easier to tackle. Mere conditions get juiced up into diseases by highly paid public-relations departments, and rare illnesses are pushed as being on the increase.

Everyday traits such as shyness grow into sicknesses. Roche developed the drug Manerix to treat 'social phobia', and claimed that one million Australians suffered from it. But the company could not initially find enough sufferers for clinical trials. That was a few years back. Now, social phobia is becoming increasingly accepted as a condition. Pfizer markets the drug Zoloft in America as a cure for Social Anxiety Disorder. Yep, SAD.

New technology has boosted our lust for scary info about illnesses. Health is now the second most popular internet search topic, after pornography. Doctors call it cyberchondria. People with minor everyday snuffles Google their symptoms and strike an oozing seam of illness. Indigestion, say the websites, could be stomach cancer, headaches might be a brain tumour, those pins and needles could mean multiple sclerosis.

The final culprits in stoking up modern hypochondria are people like me, who work in the information industry. Readers want to pore over newly discovered threats to their health and sanity, and journalists are perfectly happy to oblige – often by rewriting drug companies' overblown press releases with a cynically uncritical eye.

Two London community-health experts complained in the *British Medical Journal* on 28 February 2004, that in the previous month alone they had read newspaper reports about studies that 'proved' that moving to the countryside, drinking wine or discussing your relationship problems in bed can improve sexual problems. They also read that owning a pet helps you recover more quickly from illness, testosterone causes unsafe sex and texting is good for your mental health.

But it's all a load of public-relations eyewash, they say: 'PR companies have big budgets to promote their research, to the exclusion of more reliable, ethical work. Often the PR company has decided on the outcome way before the study begins. Because PR survey results are presented as startling, journalists may see a good headline, a light story, or a way of meeting a looming deadline.'

And the Oxford-based Social Issues Research Centre recently attacked the media's habit of raising false hopes by publicizing medical breakthroughs that do not exist. 'There must come a time when excessive, unfounded hyping, often amounting to nothing more than cruel hoaxes, is curtailed,' it says. Some hope. Who wants a bunch of complicated stats and facts to ruin a good yarn?

But in spite of all this, we should not feel bad about our modern-day mass neurosis. That could cause an epidemic of Hyperchondriasis Denial Syndrome to afflict millions of highly vulnerable health addicts. Instead we should take the chance to celebrate the masterpiece of human creativity that is hypochondria.

What follows is the result of my squirreling hundreds of daft, disturbing, rare, strange, spurious, wacko and sometimes plain disgusting health-research reports into a desk drawer while spending the past decade as a health journalist. From this medical mulch has grown a monument to the hypochondriacal human condition.

It is also a tribute to hard work – in the shape of druggists' hype, quacks' creativity, researchers' resourcefulness, journalists' craven sensationalism – and, of course, the sheer paranoid pleasure that we all take in swallowing it all on a daily basis.

Taken en masse, this overdose of doom might even be sufficient to make right-thinking people decide to give up obsessing about their health and instead get on with living a neurosis-free life in the safest era that humanity has ever known. Now that, ultimately, would be a massive achievement for medical science.

IMPORTANT NOTE

Clinical studies show that hypochondria can kill (see page 21) – and people who fret are more likely to develop cancer and Alzheimer's disease (page 125). Please remember at all times not to let any of the information in this book worry you. Try taking it all with a pinch of salt. Not too much salt, mind.

References explained: want to know more (or just plain don't believe it)? Most entries are referenced from medical journals. The system is this: an entry such as (2002, 15; 167: 1104) translates as (year, volume; issue number: page number). Volume numbers are sometimes not given.

HOME COMFORTS

For hypochondria begins at home

TELEPHONE STROKE

Look out chatterboxes: if you love to spend hours on the phone you risk giving yourself a debilitating stroke, warns the *Canadian Medical Association Journal* (2002, 10; 167: 1104).

Dr Malvinder Parmar, the medical director of Timmins and District Hospital in Northern Ontario, says he discovered 'telephone stroke' after examining a 63-year-old man who had developed slurred speech, unsteadiness and weakness on his left side straight after finishing a 56-minute phone call.

He had suffered an obstruction of his blood flow, which Dr Parmar says was most probably caused by a crucial artery getting compressed during the phone call, when the victim had kept his head bent to the right side. The doctor says that to avoid such an injury, you should play safe and change sides often, or think about using a hands-free set at home. Or just talk less.

Dr Parmar adds telephone stroke to medicine's list of similar conditions caused by neck-benders such as chiropractic manipulation, protracted dental work, X-ray positioning and ...

BEAUTY PARLOUR SYNDROME

Vanity can come at a crippling price, and not only at the make-up counter. Beauty parlour syndrome was identified by Michael Weintraub, of the New York Medical College, Valhalla. He was alerted to the perils of keeping up appearances after seeing five female patients admitted to hospital suffering from strokes that occurred after they had gone for a shampoo and set.

The women, aged from 54 to 84, left the parlours with a range of stroke-like symptoms, from vertigo to partial paralysis. Weintraub believes they suffered injuries to the arteries carrying blood to the brain when their heads were stretched backwards over the hairdressers' sinks. He sent a message to parlour-owners in the *Journal of the American Medical Association* (1993, 269; 16: 2086): go easy on older clients, lest they curl and die.

HANDKERCHIEF OF GRIEF

Should Kleenex carry a health warning? **Vigorous nose-blowing** can in rare cases create a blast of internal pressure so powerful it will crack your orbit, the bony cavity in which the eye sits. And that may lead to serious trouble, doctors warn.

Hard nose-blowing will force air through a fractured eye socket into the skull, where it can cause subcutaneous emphysema – air trapped in tissues where air should not be, say doctors at Birmingham City Hospital. They report how one 20-year-old woman managed to blast so much air through her broken eye socket that it ended up in her chest cavity, causing significant pain, in the *Journal of Laryngology & Otology* (2003, 117; 2: 141).

Over-enthusiastic honking can potentially cause blindness, because of the possible effects of air pressure and infection, warn doctors at Craigavon Area Hospital, Northern Ireland, in the same publication (2001, 115; 4: 319). More comfortingly, though, they say that often the fracture will spontaneously repair itself in around two weeks.

DEAFENING BLOW

It is not only the eyes and chest that are imperilled by vigorous hankie use. Japanese doctors from Kawanishi Municipal Hospital report how one 55-year-old man suffered blower's deafness in both ears after a good old blast into his handkerchief. He gradually developed vertigo and then his left eyeball started oscillating. The eye trouble and vertigo cleared up, but a year later his hearing had not improved, says the case study in the *Nippon Jibiinkoka Gakkai Kaiho* (1997, 100; 11: 1375). The medics say the damage was caused by the patient over-pressurizing his inner ears.

Some people just ask for trouble, though. German doctors report in *Laryngorhinootologie* (1992, 71; 9: 485) how another patient achieved much the same injury by trying to inflate a party balloon with his nose.

MONEY WORRIES?

If you have an aversion to meeting the bank manager, it might not simply be down to the parlous state of your finances. You could have a real illness.

Researchers at Cambridge University claim to have discovered a psychological condition they call **financial phobia**. They say that it affects more than nine million people in Britain.

Sufferers become seized with anxiety, guilt or boredom when confronted with the need to manage their money. They resort to avoidance techniques such as not checking bank balances and, in extreme cases, throwing away unopened statements. Nearly half of a sample of a thousand otherwise well-adjusted people polled experienced a racing heart when faced with managing money: 15 per cent said they felt immobilized, 12 per cent felt physically ill and 11 per cent went all dizzy.

Brendan Burchell, a senior lecturer in social and political sciences, says in the *Guardian* (27 January 2003) that financial phobia affects 20 per cent of the population, particularly women and young people. Nearly a third of those asked said they would rather visit the dentist than sit down with a bank statement.

FASHION VICTIMS

Those trousers a bit snug? Waddling about in skin-tight strides not only makes you look ridiculous, it could also land you in dire straits. Octavio Bessa, of Stanford, Connecticut, reports how he kept seeing patients with mystery stomach pains that modern medical diagnostics could not explain.

He realized that the patients had recently put on weight, but had not invested in larger clothes. 'I noticed that the difference between these patients' abdominal girth measurement and pants size is usually 7.5cm (3in). All the symptoms disappear after the use of braces and a change in pants size,' he says in the *Archives of Internal Medicine* (1993, 153; 11: 1396). 'I have coined this the **tight pants syndrome**.'

Dr Deborah Allen of the Indiana University School of Medicine, Indianapolis, replied to Bessa, saying that overweight patients often show signs of hiatus hernias, which disappear under examination. Because they've removed the offending trousers.

TRUCKER'S TROUSER

Similar problems appear among those notorious fashion victims – truck drivers. 'Most of them are obese and wear tight-fitting denims,' says Dr J.R. Boyce of the University of Alabama in Birmingham. He reports in the *Journal of the American Medical Association* (1984, 251; 12: 1553) that, 'A number of truck drivers who consented to wearing loose-fitting, albeit less fashionable, trousers had notable improvement of their symptoms.'

HIPSTER HELL

Still more trouser-related trauma has been blamed on hipster pants coming into fashion. These can cause mystery burning sensations in the thighs (those of the wearers, not onlookers).

Malvinder Parmar, the medical director at Timmins & District Hospital, Ontario, Canada, says he encountered three 'mildly obese young women' between the ages of 22 and 35, who had worn tight low-rise trousers over the previous six to eight months. All had symptoms of tingling or burning sensations on the side of the thigh.

One of the women was becoming convinced she had multiple sclerosis and wanted an MRI scan, but Parmar decided that pressure on her lateral femoral cutaneous nerve was the problem, and her hipsters were the cause. His prescription, in the *Canadian Medical Association Journal* (2003, 168; 1: 16), was for her to wear loose-fitting dresses – far more ladylike.

LINGERIE DEPARTMENT

The **G-string**, the modern way to avoid the dreaded visible panty line, is blamed for causing health troubles, too. The skimpy knickers have been fingered for causing chronic infections such as cystitis. Marks & Spencer says the thong is its hottest-selling women's lingerie item in Britain, but the *Patient's Encyclopedia of Cystitis* warns that many designs have hard seams that can irritate the vaginal area and the string can transfer bacteria from the bottom. Sexy.

That other modern lingerie phenomenon, the **push-up bra**, has also been criticized by medical experts who claim that constricting brassières can cause back pain. In 1995, the medical anthropologist Sydney Singer claimed tight bras may cause congestion in the lymph nodes. He argues that breast cancer is a problem only among cultures where women wear bras.

The British School of Osteopathy doesn't like push-up bras either. It says they may be linked to a wide range of health problems such as breathing difficulties and spinal pain, and even side-effects such as constipation and irritable bowel syndrome.

UNDONE BY FLIES

Males live in peril of their clothes, too. How many guys have been undone by their flies? Researchers can only guess that most men have suffered **penile zip injury**. Most often it is a trauma suffered in childhood – just one of life's more painful little lessons. Scottish casualty consultants report in *Injury* (1994, 25; 1: 59) that one in every 4,000 new patients is a trouser-trapped child.

But plenty of men forget that important formative lesson, says Richard Hockey, the data analyst at Australia's Queensland Injury Surveillance Unit. He found that trapped genitals are far and away the leading cause of clothing-related injury when he analysed emergency-department statistics from 1998 to 2001.

'People probably try to treat themselves first. The embarrassment factor might put you off seeking help as long as possible,' he says in the *Medical Post* (8 October 2002). 'Maybe it is seasonal. In the hotter weather, anecdotally, people are going without underpants.'

Medical science is split on the best course of action. New York doctors in *Pediatric Emergency Care* (1993, 9; 2: 90) suggest you can free fly-trapped men by pouring mineral oil over the zip, while across the Atlantic, researchers in *European Urology* (1981, 7; 6: 365) suggest cutting across the zip where it has pinched the foreskin. Others suggest a rapid yank downwards should do the trick.

Old-fashioned button flies might be the best long-term answer.

WALLET WARNING

One further cause of male trouser trauma: Elmar Lutz of St Mary's Hospital, New Jersey, reports two cases of patients suffering mysterious painful thighs and lower backs – one had lasted 14 months, the other eight years. Slipped discs had been investigated, chiropractors visited, but to no avail.

The answer, Lutz realized, is the previously unknown danger of sitting on a fat wallet for great lengths of time. One patient's wallet was more than 1in thick and contained a small library of credit cards.

In each case, **credit card sciatica** was cured by 'the simple procedure of a walletectomy', says Lutz in the *Journal of the American Medical Association* (1978, 240; 8: 738). Relief was 'fairly immediate'.

'I have encountered several other cases over the years and this tends to indicate that the problem is more common than realized,' he says. 'If unrelieved, it could lead to eventually more severe neurovascular dysfunction and nerve injury.' Luckily the doctors are there to help empty your purse.

BIBLIO-PILES

Please don't leave this book in the bathroom. Reading on the loo can give you haemorrhoids, warns an article in the *Lancet* (1989, 1; 8628: 54). Doctors at the John Radcliffe Hospital, Oxford, compared the habits of 100 people suffering from haemorrhoids with 100 unaffected people and found that a much larger proportion of the group suffering from haemorrhoids reads on the loo. Reading in itself is not bad for you; but sitting on the lavatory for long periods causes undue pressure on your bottom, say the Oxford doctors.

HOUSEWORK MASSACRES MEN

DIY might better be spelt DYI – Do Yourself In – if we are to believe figures showing that men have a ten-times higher risk of death per minute spent doing home maintenance than women, and even manage a four-times greater risk of suffering a fatality when performing simple housework.

The statistics, culled from coroners' files in Australia over a three-year period, show what dangerous places homes can be if you are male. Men represent 83 per cent of home-death victims. The study found that the most common items involved in deaths were ladders (18 per cent), collapsing car jacks (7 per cent) and portable electric cables (5 per cent). Many of the deaths were remarkably similar, say the researchers in the journal *Injury Prevention* (2003, 9; 1: 15).

They were:

- *'Persons (usually male) performing maintenance on cars which were inadequately jacked up and which rolled or fell on them, causing death through crush asphyxia or head injuries.'*
- *'Persons (usually male) performing maintenance on the home with faulty equipment or without ensuring the relevant electrical circuits had been isolated.'*
- *'Persons (usually male) killed in fires started as a result of leaving the stove turned on after cooking or leaving something cooking while they fell asleep.'*

Play safe, guys. Get a woman to do it.

IT'S A JUNGLE OUT THERE

Gardening equipment most frequently involved in injuries:

Lawnmowers
Secateurs, pruning clippers and shears
Hedge-trimmers
Spades, shovels and garden forks
Saws
Stepladders
Ladders
Strimmers

(Source: *UK Home Accident Surveillance Statistics*, 2000)

That's just the obvious stuff, though. More than 1,000 people a year in Britain are injured by wheelbarrows. And about 400 manage to have an accident involving a trowel.

DISHCLOTH DISEASE

That innocent-looking dishcloth could be wiping you out. A UK study covered by the International Scientific Forum on Home Hygiene says 84 per cent of dish-cloths are contaminated with the food-poisoning bacterium, listeria. The Forum says you can get up to 1 million bacteria on your hands just by wringing out an infected sponge or dishrag.

Meanwl ile, Charles Gerba and his team at Arizona University in Tucson inspected dishcloths across the US and concluded that they are making countless people ill. The microbiologists collected dishcloths and sponges from 100 homes in each of five big cities, and found that some sort of pathogen lurked in 70 per cent of them. Twenty per cent harboured salmonella and staphylococcus, the most common causes of food-borne illness in America, Gerba says in *New Scientist* (2 September 1995).

DON'T TOUCH THAT DOORKNOB

One doorhandle contaminated with harmful bacteria or viruses can infect at least the first 14 people who touch it, according to German researchers in the *Journal of Hospital Infection* (2000, 46: 61). That may be enough to cause household panic, because doorknobs, along with bathroom taps, toilet flushes and soap dispensers, are the most common ways you can pick up viral contamination passed on by someone who didn't wash their hands after using the loo, according to a 2001 study for *Social Science and Medicine*.

There is apparently no escape: simply flushing the loo after an episode of diarrhoea can infect the toilet seat, lid and the surrounding air with infectious bacteria that may hang around in the toilet water for up to 50 days, reports the *Journal of Applied Microbiology* (2000, 89: 137).

OR MAYBE WE SHOULD GET DIRTY

Then again, there's the hygiene hypothesis, which argues that more and more children are developing asthma because they have not been exposed to dirt and bacteria early on. This is based on studies such as that in the *Deutsch Medical Wochenschreib* (2000, 125;

31–32: 923) which followed 1,300 children for 16 years and found that those brought up on farms had a much lower incidence of asthma than infants raised in fastidious urban homes.

The scientists suspect that the lack of 'environmental insults' deprive the urban children's immune systems of the early stimuli that encourage them to develop fully. The lack of exposure to our natural grubby environment may mean they have pernickety defences that can't tell the difference between threatening substances and harmless ones.

BUT THEN AGAIN ...

Indoor pollution can endanger health more than pollution encountered outdoors, argue scientists in a European Union-commissioned report released in September 2003. High cancer and allergy rates are linked to constant exposure to harmful gases and chemicals from household goods, according to the Euro-doomsters.

The EU report says that cigarette smoke and items such as computers, carpets, paints and plastics all release toxic chemicals. It argues that the incidence of asthma, now reportedly suffered by one in five Britons, has been linked to the damaging effects of indoor air.

SPECTACLES OF DEATH

Still more indoor perils, this time for short-sighted people: wearing metal-framed spectacles could put you at risk of night blindness or even eye cancer, warns Pat Thomas, the author of the 2003 book, *Living Dangerously: Are Everyday Toxins Making You Sick?* She claims that metal spectacle frames can act as focussing antennae for electro-magnetic forces from computers, electric toothbrushes, microwave ovens, power points, vacuum cleaners and toasters – in fact, pretty much anything with a plug on it. Ever felt threatened by a toaster before? She claims that the risk is known to the World Health Organization.

KILLER CANDLES

Thomas is not the most relaxing person to have around the house: she also warns that candles can create clouds of dangerous chemicals. She quotes researchers in the *Journal of the American Medical Association* (2000, 284; 2: 180) who bought candles from 12 different stores and found that a third had metallic candles – and one tenth of these contained lead. The metal is still used by some candlemakers to stiffen candlewicks. 'Every time you burn one of these lead-containing candles, you release significant amounts of neurotoxic lead into the atmosphere,' Thomas says.

A further study in *Scientific Total Environment* (2002, 296; 1–3: 159) warns that burning more than one candle in a room can push airborne-lead levels above US safety limits. There goes that romantic dinner.

INDOOR SCLEROSIS

If that weren't enough to get you out of the house: staying indoors could help to end your life. We all know the manifold warnings about going out in the sun and getting skin cancer, but Australian researchers based at the University of Tasmania claim that the more sun you had as a child, the lower your chances of developing multiple sclerosis.

They compared 136 people with multiple sclerosis with 272 randomly drawn people of similar ages, and found that those who had been out in the sun more than two to three hours a day between the ages of six and 15 had a significantly lower risk of MS. Higher exposure in winter seemed more important than higher exposure in summer. They concluded in the *British Medical Journal* (2003, 327; 7410: 316) that insufficient ultraviolet light may influence the development of the potentially fatal progressive disease.

SHADE-LOVER'S CARCINOMA

Avoiding the sun can also make you more vulnerable to a range of cancers which kill more than 38,000 Britons a year, claims Professor Cedric Garland of the University of California.

He recommends that you try to get some sun every day to allow adequate build-up of vitamin D, which reduces the risk of colon, breast, prostate and other cancers. Professor Garland says in the *British Medical Journal* (2003, 327; 7425: 1228), 'Advice to avoid the sun would not be the best strategy for reducing overall incidence of cancer.'

He advises, for example, that UK residents aim for ten to 15 minutes a day in the sun when the weather allows, without sunscreen, to allow adequate synthesis of vitamin D. He adds, 'People in the UK cannot synthesise vitamin D from November to the end of March, [so] they become deficient by December.'

HOW WILL YOU DIE?

(Venomous spider or firework accident, the odds are the same)

Your odds for meeting the Grim Reaper via:

Complications of hospital care:	one in 1,170
Riding a motorbike:	one in 1,295
Fatal air accident:	one in 4,608
Being accidentally shot:	one in 4,613
Tripping over on level ground:	one in 6,336
Falling off a ladder:	one in 8,689
Choking on your own vomit:	one in 9,372
Driving in a heavy truck:	one in 9,702
Drowning in the bath:	one in 10,948
Suffocating in bed:	one in 10,948
Scalded by hot tap water:	one in 65,092
Hornet, wasp or bee stings:	one in 66,297
In a three-wheeled vehicle:	one in 155,654
On foot:	one in 610
Fireworks:	one in 716,010
Venomous spiders:	one in 716,010

(Source: American National Safety Council's *Lifetime Risk of Death Study*, 2000)

ON THE OTHER HAND ...

Rail journey less risky than asteroid collision (but only just)

If the American scale were not precise enough, science has created another system to help us mortals fixate on our inevitable demise. Frank Duckworth, the eminent statistician and editor of the *Royal Statistical Society News*, has used figures from the *British Medical Journal* and the UK Health and Safety Executive to create the 'Riskometer' (a name that cries out to be prefixed with the word Acme) to measure the risks of everyday living.

Like the Richter scale for earthquakes, and the Beaufort scale for wind, the Duckworth Riskometer is a logarithmic scale. This means things get much, much more dangerous the higher you go up the numerical rankings. Zero indicates simply living on the earth for one year; slightly more risky is taking a 160km train journey, rated at 0.3; at 8.0 is playing a game of Russian roulette with a full chamber.

RISKOMETER RATINGS

8.0   Suicide; Russian roulette (with six bullets); jumping off Eiffel Tower; lying in front of an express train

7.2   Russian roulette (one game, one bullet)

7.1   Continuing to smoke cigarettes (male aged 35, 40 a day)

6.9   Continuing to smoke cigarettes (male aged 35, 20 a day)

6.7   Continuing to smoke cigarettes (male aged 35, 10 a day)

6.4   Deep sea fishing (40-year career)

6.3   Rock climbing (over 20 years)

5.5   Accidental falls (newborn male)

5.5   Lifetime car travel (newborn male); dying
       while vacuuming, washing up, walking down
       the street
4.6   Murder (newborn male over whole lifetime)
4.2   Rock-climbing (one session)
1.9   160km car journey (sober middle-aged driver)
1.7   1600km flight
1.6   Asteroid impact in the lifetime of a newborn
       male
0.3   160km rail journey

Why are vacuuming the carpet and washing the dishes more risky than rock-climbing? It's about the relative amount of time you spend doing them, says
Duckworth: 'I guess the risk of death in a lifetime of
carrying out household chores would be between 4
and 6 on the scale.' As for asteroids and rail journeys,
best keep a wary eye out of the carriage window for
rogue space rocks.

PHONE-STRIKE FATALITIES

Fifteen-year-old Alex Derrick was talking to his girlfriend on the phone on Boxing Night, when he had a
terrible shock. No, she hadn't chucked him. He was
struck by phone-conducted lightning. 'I heard a rumble of thunder, then a big bang and I saw the fuse box
blow and a huge spark came at me. I then dropped the
phone as I felt a very warm sensation up my arm,'
says Derrick.

It could happen to you. Electricity experts suggest
in the *Western Daily Press* (29 December 1999) that
lightning had hit the telephone wire connected to
Derrick's home, causing a high-voltage bolt of power
to shoot along the phone line. He suffered a serious

shock but walked away unharmed, thanks to the fact that he was wearing rubber-soled shoes.

Phone-conducted lightning is not particularly rare. When the 17-year-old New York student Jason Findley was found lying on a bed with a receiver at his ear, investigators concluded that he had been electrocuted when lightning blasted an electrical surge through the telephone wire into his left ear and caused his heart to stop, reports the *New York Times* (16 February 1986).

Officials of New Jersey Bell Telephone Company say telephone-related strikes are not uncommon, but fatal accidents are unusual. Several weeks before Findley's death, a New Jersey man was found unconscious with the phone in his hand after having received an electrical jolt. He survived.

In 2001, the *Journal of Laryngology & Otology* (2001, 115; 1: 4) reported 18 cases of ear injuries caused by lightning seen at the University Hospital of Split, in Croatia, between 1984 and 1999. Not surprisingly, all were admitted complaining of 'severe pain, tinnitus [ringing in the ears] and hearing impairment'. Twelve of them suffered ruptured ear drums, though all were treated successfully. 'Lightning survivors require additional psychotherapeutic treatment,' the doctors recommend.

Dr Christopher Andrews, of Queensland, Australia, agrees about the need for mind therapy. He says about 80 people a year in Australia receive shocks from lightning surges while using telephones, and adds in the *Medical Journal of Australia* (1993, 157; 11–12: 823) that victims do not only need care for shock and burns. They may require treatment with anti-depressants, as there is a strong element of 'no one else seems to understand' involved. Phone-strike survivors don't get much sympathy – their friends tend to fall about laughing.

MOULD MANIA

Noticed any spots of fungus in your house? Prepare to panic. Parts of America have become gripped by mould-allergy mania, after Melinda Ballard and her husband Ron Allison won a $32 million compensation in 2001 for a claim that their home had been infected by black mould which caused Allison to experience memory loss and their son to suffer asthma and seizures.

Mould-affected homeowners across the nation panicked and left their homes. Mould-claim payouts jumped to $1 billion in three years. A government agency, the Centre for Disease Control, initially decreed that mould might cause bleeding in infants' lungs. It later changed its mind.

Ms Ballard's lawsuit judgment was reduced on appeal to $4 million compensation – not for mould compensation, but as punitive damages for the insurance company's foot-dragging over the case. The trial judge excluded all medical evidence of mould's health effects because the science behind it seemed unsound.

Nevertheless, the mould scare looks set to rumble on. 'How to spot mould illness' articles are starting to become regulars in the medical press, and the Texas State Bar Association now holds an Annual Advanced Mould Litigation Course.

'Five years ago, we would get one call a month about mould,' says Robert Krell, the president of IAQ Technologies, an indoor environmental consulting company in Syracuse, New York. 'Now we get ten calls a day. I've seen people make themselves ill with hysteria.'

Dan Sitomer, an attorney specializing in mould litigation, tells ABC News (23 March 2004), 'From the moment that a building is viewed as a mould problem, its value goes to zero. The litigation is so aggressive and has multiplied so quickly that it has frightened the insurance industry. The damages claims can include almost anything. Pain and suffering, negligence, the claims just go on and on.'

Now most US insurance companies will not cover damages related to mould, reports ABC news. But not everyone is convinced about the danger. 'Mould illnesses are all hypotheses that need to be studied more,' Dr Robert Haley, the head of epidemiology at the University of Texas Southwestern Medical Center, has told the *Texas Monthly*. 'But for now, it sounds like a lot of people went and got diagnosed by their lawyers.'

HYPOCHONDRIA
CAN KILL

Like you didn't have enough to fret about

If you are worried sick about your health, then you may be right to fret – you could fall victim of the **nocebo effect**. It is the placebo effect's evil dark-side brother. A placebo makes you get better because it helps you believe you will get better. The nocebo effect makes people who worry about illness become ill. And thus, paradoxically, it proves that hypochondria really isn't all in the mind.

Doctors have known about the placebo effect for thousands of years. Convince a person that some substance will make them recover from illness, and there is a strong chance it will do the trick – even if medically it doesn't actually work. Nowadays, the placebo pill used in medical drug trials – normally just a taste-free sugar tablet – can achieve a cure in anything up to 40 per cent of the people who take it. This can prove rather embarrassing if the expensive new wonder pill being tested against it doesn't do any better.

For many years, doctors have debated whether to work on 'harnessing the placebo effect', but time after time they have backed off because it makes their scientific professional cred look a bit witch-doctory. Placebo is all about harnessing the power of the mind, something that can't be measured, packaged and sold – not least because it's so hit-and-miss. And doctors don't do voodoo, at least not officially.

The medical professions speak even less of the nocebo effect – probably because it is so spooky – and also because it gives hypochondriacs something real to complain about. In one example of nocebo, researchers discovered that women who believe they are prone to heart disease are nearly four times as likely to die as women with similar risk factors who don't hold such fatalistic views.

The study, reported in the *Journal of the American Medical Association* (1996, 275; 5: 345), covered more than 5,000 women in Framingham, Massachusetts, a town whose population has been studied since 1948 in a long-term examination of three generations of Americans. The study results reinforced medics' understanding of the nocebo phenomenon, which was first identified more than four decades ago.

Nocebo (from the Latin 'I will harm') seems a cruel testimony to the power of human imagination. 'People are convinced that something is going to go wrong, and it is a self-fulfilling prophecy,' says Arthur J. Barsky, a psychiatrist at Boston's Brigham and Women's Hospital, who warns in the *Journal of the American Medical Association* (2002, 287; 5: 622) that doctors must pay closer attention to the nocebo effect. 'From a clinical point of view, this is by no means peripheral or irrelevant,' he says.

Barsky's round-up of previous studies shows how 16 years ago, researchers at three medical centres undertook a study of aspirin and another blood thinner in heart patients and discovered that warning the aspirin-takers about possible side-effects increased the number of patients who suffered them.

At two of the medical centres, patients were told of possible stomach problems, one of the most common side-effects of repeated use of aspirin. At the other location, patients received no warning. The patients warned about the gastrointestinal trouble were almost three times as likely to suffer from it.

Another study, in the July 1981 *Pavlovian Journal of Biological Sciences* (sign on front door, 'Please knock: doorbell makes secretary dribble') reports how more than two-thirds of a random sample of 34 college students reported mild headaches when told that a non-existent electric current was passing through their heads.

Barsky has profiled the type of patient who is most likely to experience the nocebo effect of worse side-effects and poorer results on a given drug. When he sees a patient with a history of vague, difficult-to-diagnose complaints who is sure that whatever therapy is prescribed will do little to battle their problem, he says, those low expectations are almost inevitably met. The treatments usually fail.

COURT-CASE CRIPPLES

The nocebo effect also blights victims of accidents who become embroiled in long-running legal cases in pursuit of damages. This sub-set of the nocebo world has its own title, **compensation neurosis**. Sadly, the process of going through the courts means they never get better – especially if they win their case.

'Results of medical treatment are notoriously poor in patients with pending litigation after personal injury or disability claims', says a report in *Clinical Orthopedics* (1997, 336: 94). These people are not malingering, it stresses. It is just that all the courtroom drama convinces their subconscious brains to ensure they stay wounded. 'Adversarial administrative and legal systems challenging the claimant to prove repeatedly that they are permanently ill harden the conviction of illness,' the American report explains.

Worse still, even getting a fat cheque at the end of the case does not help: 'Because any improvement in the claimant's health condition may result in denial of disability status in the future, the complainant is compelled to guard against getting well and is left with no honourable way to recover from illness.'

CULTURAL CRASHES

All this could well explain why, if you want to avoid **whiplash** injury, you should not crash your car in Canada. Have the same neck-spraining accident in Greece instead. The Greeks don't have a culture of making insurance claims for whiplash after car crashes – and neither do they suffer any of the common whiplash claimants' long-term disabling symptoms, say reports from Alberta University, Canada.

The researchers wanted to discover why whiplash injuries are endemic in Canada but almost unknown in Greece. They asked Canadians and Greeks to imagine what injuries they would get from a neck-twisting motor wreck. Half the Canadians said they might suffer long-term disability, but almost none of the Greeks did, says the report in the *Medical Science Monitor* (2003, 3: CR 120–4).

What is behind the huge difference in expectations? It is the chance of winning a big compensation payout in litigious Western countries such as Canada, says another Alberta University report, in *Orthopade* (2001, 30; 8: 551). 'In countries where whiplash syndrome does not exist, accident victims do not routinely hear reports of how it can cause severe long-term disability, so don't expect it can happen to them,' the researchers say.

'They do not engage in a process that encourages hypervigilance for symptoms. They also do not engage in a process that engineers anxiety, frustration, and resentment from battling with insurance companies and proving that your pain is real. They will not amplify daily life's aches and pains. They will not attribute all these different sources of symptoms to chronic damage they believe the accident caused.'

LOVE AND SEX

Is that Cupid's arrow, or has the Grim Reaper taken up archery?

MISTRESS DISTRESS

Illicit relationships can kill you. Professor Graham Jackson, a consultant at St Thomas' Hospital in London, claims that three-quarters of sudden deaths during sex happen to people who are having affairs. This is particularly true of older people, says Jackson.

British statistics show that one per cent of sudden deaths occur during sex, but you can boost your chances of a fatality by having more intercourse – with young and illicit partners. Jackson told a conference of the European Society for Sexual and Impotence Research in Hamburg (December 2002) that older, married men having flings with younger mistresses are particularly at risk.

If that were not potentially embarrassing enough, a study of 37 sex-related fatalities between 1972 and 1992, reported in Germany's *Zeitschrift für Kardiologie* (1999, 88; 1: 44), found the majority had died of a heart attack and, 'in most cases sudden death occurred during the sexual act with a prostitute'.

The phenomenon of illicit-sex-related deaths may be explained by clinical studies that claim to demonstrate that adultery works your heart harder than marital intercourse, which in turn is more stressful than masturbation.

The 'sexologist', Dr Alan Riley claims that heart rate increases by around 30 per cent during intercourse, and by a maximum of 120 per cent during orgasm. Masturbation, meanwhile, increases heart rate by around 29 per cent, reaching a maximum increase of only 57 per cent at orgasm.

In a 1983 study he reports how a 44-year-old man who had sex with both his wife and his mistress in the same day found that his heart recorded 92 beats per minute making love to his wife, and a high of 150bpm with his mistress. (But who was taking his pulse?) It may perhaps be no surprise to learn that the subject was supposed to be recuperating from a heart attack at the time.

Philanderers seeking to evade this cardiac curse might try asking their partners to go on top. But, according to Dr Riley, position makes very little difference to the rate of cardiac exertion. Either way, men should expect on average to expend a similar level of energy to that used when playing golf while carrying the clubs. Except that golfers don't expect to go home with an empty bag after playing a round.

SEXY WIFE SHOCK

Ditch that attractive partner. Men with ugly wives live up to 12 years longer because they are not worried about them being unfaithful, Yale University scientists claimed in 1999 after studying the survival rates of several hundred couples.

Press reports give no information as to how the researchers rated the wives scientifically for attractiveness or ugliness. Perhaps they used the MilliHelen scale, where 1MH is equivalent to the amount of beauty required to launch one ship. The Yale psychologist Edgar

Dablen says, 'Men with attractive women are permanently jealous. They are always seeing competition, which is an unhealthy and stressful situation.'

DANGERS OF DISSENT

Men, it seems, are immune to nagging – but their wives' lives could be in peril from frequent disagreements. Psychologists at Ohio State University studied 31 couples who were married for an average of 42 years, and found that wives' stress-hormone levels rose significantly at times when marital strife had been increased by partners' criticizing, interrupting and disapproving.

The study, by Janice Kiecolt-Glaser and colleagues in *Psychosomatic Medicine* (1997, 59: 339), found that the men's levels appeared unchanged. Perhaps they weren't listening.

Maybe if you are a man the damage is primarily physical rather than emotional. A study by accident and emergency doctors in Sunderland found a significant number of men had punched their hands through windows following arguments with their partners. Seventy per cent of them did it between the hours of 11 p.m. and 4 a.m. More than half had to be hospitalized.

INFLATABLE WOMAN WARNING

A new trend for giving women blow-jobs may well reflect true sexual equality, but it also seems responsible for increasing numbers of women suffering mysterious chest pains, warn V.R. Jacobs and colleagues in the *Journal of the Society of Laporoendoscopic Surgeons* (2000, 4; 4: 297).

They focus on the case of an otherwise young and

healthy woman who arrived at the emergency department of Stanford University, California, complaining of recurrent chest pains. When X-rayed, she was found to have air under her diaphragm, where air shouldn't be. The condition is called pneumoperitoneum, and is usually caused by a perforated bowel or by surgeons accidentally letting air into the body during an operation.

But both those causes were quickly ruled out. The medics, in true baffled-doctor mode, resorted to asking the woman about her lovemaking habits. She finally admitted to a liking for **vaginal insufflation** – having her boyfriend blow up her for all he was worth.

This is a rather perilous form of blowjob, though. 'Patients are often unaware of the open access between the vagina and the abdomen,' says Jacobs. 'Vaginal insufflation can dilate genital organs and push remarkable amounts of air into the abdomen. It can take several days for the body to absorb the air, and the patient often does not connect the pain with its cause.'

You don't necessarily need a man to do it, either. French pathologists report the tragic case of a woman who killed herself by vaginal insufflation while masturbating. Their report, in the *International Journal of Legal Medicine* (1990, 104; 1: 59), says the 40-year-old woman was using a carrot as a dildo when, bicycle-pump-style, she managed to push enough air into herself to introduce a lethal embolism – a bubble of gas – into her bloodstream.

The pathologists, based in Garches, say the case appears unprecedented, but speculate that this might be down to the fact that investigators do not look for it as a cause of death. They say it may also be that victims' partners deny that any dangerous behaviour was going on.

LEG-CROSSER'S IMPOTENCE

Look out men, you risk infertility if you don't keep your knees apart. Professor Marc Goldstein says leg-crossing can lower a man's sperm production.

The professor of urology and director of the Center for Male Reproductive Medicine in New York says that sitting with one leg flung over the other for 20 minutes raises the temperature of the testes from around 32°C, the optimum temperature for sperm-making, to between 36°C and 37°C. That could, he says, lower a man's fertility, though it won't show for 11 weeks, the Center points out, because it takes the body 77 days to create sperm.

'Temperature is a very important factor in testicular function, and 2,000 years ago the Japanese used hot baths as a form of contraception. Anything above the optimum temperature could be detrimental,' Professor Goldstein argues in the *Independent* (4 August 1999).

WET NIGHTMARES

Talk in your sleep? Walk in your sleep? Drive in your sleep? You could be in danger of developing **sexsomnia**, or sleep-sex, according to Colin Shapiro, the director of Toronto University's Sleep and Alertness Clinic.

He cites 11 cases of people who unwittingly performed sex acts while asleep, often with unfortunate results. They did everything from normal intercourse to downloading porn from the internet, he writes in the *Canadian Journal of Psychiatry* (2003, 48; 5: 311). The patients had been referred to the clinic for other reasons and only mentioned the problem when questioned. 'For many patients, embarrassment or a sense of guilt delayed medical enquiries,' he says. 'We anticipate that the number of potential cases is large, but sexual behaviour in sleep is not recognised by physicians and hence is not considered worthy of history-taking or meriting referral for clinical examination.'

Shapiro's cases include 'JK', a married nightclub bouncer. He was referred to Shapiro after complaints by his wife, who claimed he frequently sexually assaulted her while sleeping. Criminal charges had been laid, and she was considering leaving him. He admitted attempting cunnilingus and intercourse while he was sleeping, but said he only knew of it because she had told him about it afterwards. Our somnambulant sex-machine snored, as well as being prone to sleepwalking. When he was given an oxygen-feed device to stop his snoring, the sexual assaults stopped. So after two months he stopped wearing it. The sexual assaults began again.

'DW', a 43-year-old divorced police officer, had previously been arrested and charged with drunk driving, but was acquitted on the defence of parasomnia (the medical term for general slumber-related weirdness) – he was a frequent sleepwalker and sleep-talker, and had started going for a drive while snoozing.

Sleep driving was not the only problem, though. He had a tendency to engage in intercourse when asleep. His two current girlfriends confirmed this habit. Shapiro's report says, 'One describes him as "a different person" during those activities – apparently he is a more amorous and gentle lover and more oriented toward satisfying his partner when he is asleep.'

'KB', another police officer with a history of sleep driving (what is it with police officers?), was reported by his wife to have sleep-sex about once a month. 'His wife describes him as more aggressive and more amorous at these times than when he is awake,' the researchers report. 'She says that at these times, "There is no stopping him." However, on one occasion when he grabbed her around the neck she slapped him hard and he immediately awoke and stopped the behaviour.'

In a third example cited by the researchers, a 16-year-old male sleepwalked into his uncle and aunt's bed and began fondling his uncle's testicles. His mother reports that she had previously found him downloading porn from the internet in his sleep.

Some of us may feel particularly sceptical about this last case.

DREAM DERANGEMENT

Sexsomnia is only one part of the strange world of parasomnias. You might believe you have been sound asleep all night, but you may in fact have been walking, screaming in terror, rearranging furniture, eating bizarre food mixes or wielding weapons, say Dr Mark Mahowald and Carlos Schenck, of the Minnesota Sleep Disorders Center, in *Postgraduate Medicine* (2000, 107; 3: 145).

They videotape sleepers in the midst of bizarre behaviour such as eating raw bacon and cigarettes.

Parasomnias account for 10 per cent of sleep disorders, Mahowald says. The most common, such as sleepwalking and sleep terrors, occur in deep sleep and are caused by so-called partial or confusional arousals. Some stimulus such as a loud noise partly wakes the sleeper's brain – enough for some sufferers of **REM Behaviour Disorder** to perform complex acts such as driving a car.

Mahowald and Schenck warn that in 65 per cent of their male patients over 50, the disorder is a precursor to their developing Parkinson's disease, which only becomes apparent on average about 13 years later.

But Mahowald does not believe sexsomnia should be classified as a separate disease from other parasomnias. 'Technicians have seen it in the lab for years. It happens all the time. Most likely it's a specialized form of sleepwalking,' he tells the *New York Times Magazine* (2 February 2003).

ONES TO AVOID

Sarah, Emma, Kelly, Louise, Claire, Lisa, Rachel, Clare, Michelle, Nicola

Young British women who are prone to risky unprotected sex are more likely to be called Sarah, Emma, Kelly or Louise than any other name. Clinic doctors at a hospital in Southern England studied the attendance records of nearly 1,500 women aged 16 to 24 to find out which names cropped up most, and compiled the above list.

They compared the findings with data from the Office of Population and Censuses on the most popular names over the last 20 years. Sharon and Tracey – the two names naturally most associated with promiscuous young British women – were far down the list of women's names most frequently seen in out-patients between April 1998 and March 1999 at the genito-urinary clinic of the Royal South Hants Hospital in Southampton, Hampshire.

Sharon entered the list way down at number 30 while Tracey was at 35. Suspiciously enough, the two names were seen half as often as they could have been expected, given their overall popularity. The doctors did concede, however, that some Sharons and Traceys might have visited the clinic under pseudonyms.

AMPHIBIAN OF LOVE

Mind that French food, it could make your penis fall off. Collaborators from three universities seem to have solved a century-old medical mystery linking the consumption of frogs' legs to cases of **priapism** – painful and prolonged penile erection that might appear *Carry On* hilarious, but can be seriously bad news – it can make the penis turn black and die.

The research is the first strong evidence that frogs' legs were behind two outbreaks of priapism among French soldiers in North Africa in 1861 and 1893. French doctors describe cases of '*erections douloureuses et prolongées*' among soldiers who had recently eaten frogs' legs. Precisely how long the troops were left standing to attention is unclear.

The doctors say the symptoms resembled those seen in men who had overindulged in a drug called cantharidin – popularly known as Spanish fly – which is extracted from a beetle for its supposed aphrodisiac qualities. In one of the North African cases, physicians dissecting a local frog found its guts full of these beetles. Until this study, however, nobody had shown that frogs eating the beetles could accumulate large enough concentrations of cantharidin to cause symptoms in humans who eat the frogs.

Thomas Eisner of Cornell University has now detected such concentrations in the legs of frogs fed cantharidin-producing beetles.

Researchers report in *Chemoecology* that a meal of the cantharidin-contaminated meat could contain more than enough of the compound to cause priapism. Gorging on these legs may lead to even more serious problems. People consuming 200 to 400 grams of Spanish-fly-laden frog thighs in one meal could even risk death from cantharidin poisoning, he says.

FURTHER WARNING TO WOMANIZERS

Testicles can be the death of you, according to a study of eunuchs published in 1969 which showed that their life span was on average more than 13 years longer than that of other males. Why? The geneticist David Gems, of University College, London, has an explanation. He claims it is because if you are an intact man, you wear yourself out chasing women.

Gems found in 1997 that male nematode worms live for 20 days when left on their own, but when males were kept together their life span fell to ten days. Gems says this is due to the stress of continual competition for territory and mates. Just to make sure, he tested male worms with genetic mutations that made them less active, reports *New Scientist* (24 May 1997). They lived longest – 30 days.

Male marsupial mice live for years if they are castrated, instead of just a few sex-mad weeks when left intact. 'They spend five to 11 hours a day copulating,' he says. Among humans, it is women who live longer, but men have the genetic potential to do better if they keep themselves to themselves, he argues.

PROMISCUOUS PROSTATES

Men with interesting sex lives run a greater risk of contracting prostate cancer, according to a Swedish study. It found that while cigarettes and alcohol consumption may have little direct effect on the cancer, which kills around 9,000 Britons every year, frequent sex makes contracting the cancer more likely.

The report, in *Cancer Epidemiology Biomarkers Preview* (1996, 5; 7: 509), found that men who lost their virginities earlier and had more sexual partners seem to have a higher incidence of prostate trouble. But the cancer specialist Sven-Olof Andersson of Orebro Hospital is not prescribing therapeutic celibacy: 'We don't think it's the sexual activity in itself, it might be some type of hormonal factor that also affects sexual drive,' he says.

BREAKING CONDOM NEWS

Ooops: condom-wearing does not necessarily mean safe sex. Half the men who wear condoms have had a rubber break on them during intercourse, though their partners may very well not know, say researchers backed by the Society for the Scientific Study of Sexuality, who questioned 98 male students in 1997.

A third of the men who had experienced that worrying moment of suddenly increased sensitivity hadn't told their partners. Why not? Nearly half admitted it was because they were about to orgasm. A third said they wanted to avoid responsibility for the break. The rest thought it best not to make their partner worry. The men who didn't tell were more likely to have slept around beforehand, and to have ridden bareback when they did it, says the report in the *Journal of the American Medical Association* (1997, 278; 4: 291).

SAFE SOCKS MESSAGE

Then there's always the danger of a condom falling off inside a woman mid-sex. Australian scientists who studied prostitutes and 'amateur' condom users have discovered that this is most likely to happen if you are a young, circumcized man, and put condoms on using the conventional, manufacturer-recommended method of rolling them down the penis.

The sex researchers fail to explain why circumcision might be a factor, but they strongly recommend, in the 1984 *Reproductive Health Matters* journal, that condom-wearers pull their prophylactics up like a sock. While there is a danger of sticking your fingers through the sides, they say the pull method is much easier than rolling, and therefore more effective – even if it does make you look daft.

Condom-donning success can mean little to safe sex, though, the scientists found. Half the 400 male interviewees subscribed to the 'It's the thought that counts' school of sheath-wearing. They admitted that on at least one occasion they had taken off a condom mid-sex and finished without it. That'll fool the viruses.

RIBBED FOR SENSITIVITY

Indian doctors have discovered another potential danger from prophylactics. You could choke to death on one.

Specialists at the Jaswant Rai Speciality Hospital in Meerut spent weeks giving a 27-year-old woman a range of antibiotics and tuberculosis drugs, but to no avail. Her persistent cough and fever, which had lasted six months, would not go away. So they X-rayed her chest and found that one lung had partially collapsed around a mystery object. A video probe was popped in there, revealing an 'inverted bag-like structure'. It was removed with forceps and turned out to be an old condom.

'Detailed retrospective history confirmed accidental inhalation of the condom during fellatio,' report the doctors in the *Indian Journal of Chest Disease and Allied Science* (2004, 46; 1: 55).

INFECTION? WHAT INFECTION?

How well would you trust a foreign lover? The following figures allegedly show the likelihood of people from different nationalities admitting to their partners that they have got something nasty down there:

Austria	83 per cent
United Kingdom	80 per cent
Australia	80 per cent
France	72 per cent
Czech Republic	55 per cent
Vietnam	44 per cent
Singapore	39 per cent
Thailand	20 per cent

| Taiwan | 13 per cent |
| Malaysia | 10 per cent |

(Source: *Durex Global Survey*, December 2003)

Bear in mind, though, that this survey asked people whether they *would* tell their partners if they *did* have a disease. So the survey might just prove that Malaysians told the interviewers the truth, while many Austrians are barefaced liars.

MASTURBATION DANGERS

Go easy with those one-handed fantasies: auto-erotic asphyxiation is not an uncommon form of death – as exemplified by the British Conservative MP Stephen Milligan and, reportedly, the INXS singer Michael Hutchence – but from Germany comes a salutary caution about the use of army-surplus gear in self-sex.

Researchers writing in the *Arkiv für Kriminologie* (1997, 200; 3–4: 65) tell of a 19-year-old man who purchased an ex-airforce G-suit for the purposes of solitary pleasure. This is a pressure-suit worn by jet-fighter pilots which applies pneumatic tourniquets to parts of the body in tight high-speed turns, and thus stops blood rushing to the pilot's head or feet and causing blackouts.

Things took a strange turn with our young onanist, however. He inflated the suit with a 12-volt air compressor, covered his head with three masks and a motorcycle helmet, and managed to tie up his arms and legs. The cause of death was a massive compression of the thorax. Pity the poor soul who found him.

FATAL TRACTION

Meanwhile, men who dig masochistic masturbation are in peril of suffering lethal tractor fetishes, warn forensic scientists at Ventura County, California. They report two cases in which men used the hydraulic shovels on tractors to 'suspend themselves for masochistic stimulation'.

Mmm, those tractors can sure look pretty. 'One man developed a romantic attachment to a tractor, even giving it a name and writing poetry in its honour,' says the report in the *Journal of Forensic Science* (1994, 39; 5: 1143). He died accidentally while asphyxiating himself for pleasure by hanging himself from the machine by his neck. The forensic officers say that literature he left behind suggests he enjoyed the sense of being strangled.

The other man in the report practised bondage and cross-dressing. That will be a typical tractor driver then. He died when he accidentally became pinned to the ground under a shovel after suspending himself from it by the ankles.

Did the earth move for these guys? One thing's certain, the earth movers did for them.

TERRIBLE TURN-ON

For another auto-erotic death shock turn to the *American Journal of Forensic Medical Pathology* (2003, 24; 1: 92), where J.C. Schott and colleagues tell of an 18-year-old man wearing two brassières found dead in his bedroom by his brother. Two wet green cloths were under the brassière cups, connected to the electric mains via two metal washers and an electrical cord.

'Literature depicting nude women was found near the victim,' write the forensic officers from Kentucky

University. Autopsy revealed second- and third-degree burns of the mammary regions. Death was attributed to accidental self-electrocution.

MILK-BOTTLE BOTHER

How can you while away 17 hours with your penis trapped in a milk bottle? Ask the Japanese victim of **penile incarceration**, reported in the journal *Hinyokika Kiyo* (1988, 34; 3: 514). The 38-year-old man arrived at Osaka City University Medical School after he had trapped his penis in a milk bottle the previous evening.

Once the patient had summed up the courage to come to hospital – or decided he really needed a wee – the bottle 'was successfully removed by means of a glass cutter and hammer without any complication', report the doctors.

There must be something particularly alluring about Japanese milk bottles, though. The doctors say they know of another 56 of their countrymen who have trapped their penises in exactly the same way.

MURDER WRAP

Getting wrapped and trapped was the unlikely fate of a male auto-eroticist reported in the *American Journal of Forensic Medical Pathology* (1985, 6; 2: 151). It tells of how the victim died as a result of 'jeopardizing himself' by tightly wrapping his body in plastic food-wrapping film, with an airway out of his cocoon in the form of a snorkel tube. He was busily engaged in masturbation when he apparently lost his mouth-piece. He attempted to use a knife to cut himself out, but failed and was found suffocated.

VICE SCREAM

For something still rarer, weirder, and far more German, we return to the *Arkiv für Kriminologie* (2001, 207; 5–6: 148) and a report from Berlin's Humboldt University, titled 'An unusual autoerotic accident: **sexual pleasure from peritoneal pain**'.

It reports the unfortunate story of a 23-year-old man who got his sexual thrills by jabbing his abdomen with sharp instruments. For this purpose he clamped two knife blades into a vice suspended from a rope-pulley so that he could lower it onto himself to pierce his skin with the knife tips.

Unfortunately, one of the ropes broke and the vice with the knives fell onto the man's belly, piercing a major artery, and he bled to death. This, to the authors' knowledge, has been the first ever report of a fatal auto-erotic accident in which sexual pleasure was to be obtained from painful irritation of the peritoneum. Though you may know different.

OVERDRESSED FOR SEX

Such sexual shenanigans are not only popular with Germans and Japanese people: Australians also feature proudly in the annals of one-handed death. The Forensic Science Centre in Adelaide, South Australia, reports a series of masturbation-related fatalities in the *American Journal of Forensic Medical Pathology* (2000, 21; 1: 65).

Saddest was the case of a 46-year-old man found dead in bushland clothed in a dress, female undergarments, and seven pairs of stockings and pantyhose. The underwear had been cut to enable him to access his genitals. Unfortunately it was high summer, 39 degrees centigrade – time for a light shirt and shorts, not a wardrobe-full of women's clothing.

The victim was declared dead through hyperthermia – massive overheating of the body, due to a combination of excessive clothing and high ambient temperature, says the report. He really should have changed into something more comfortable.

BLOWN OR SUCKED?

Earlier, the journal *Pathology* (1994, 26; 3: 276) featured a report from the State Health Laboratory Services in Western Australia of an elderly man who died of ischemic heart disease, apparently while masturbating with both a vacuum cleaner and a hair dryer.

FURTHER FETISH FATALITIES

If you would give your right arm to have a powerful orgasm, you may have developed **apotemnophilia**, a fetish shared by only about 200 people around the world in which sexual gratification is derived from the removal of a limb.

It's not just bad for the patients. In 1999, an unlicensed physician who amputated a healthy leg for $15,000 to satisfy his elderly patient's apotemnophilia was sentenced to 15 years in prison after the botched operation killed the man. John Ronald Brown, 77, had been a doctor for almost 30 years until his medical licence was withdrawn in 1977 for negligence.

Brown chopped off the left leg of Philip Bondy, a 79-year-old New York apotemnophiliac, in a crude operation in Mexico, and buried the severed limb to hide the evidence. Bondy was left to recuperate in a hotel room, and died two days later of gangrene poisoning.

Meanwhile, putting your partner high up on a plinth could be dangerous if you fall off while having sex. Some people are sexually attracted to statues. They are, repeat after me, **reiphipheliacs**. The objects of their desire may be unresponsive but they are cheap to take out, and easy to seduce. 'It's the ultimate in consensual sex,' says Stephen Juan, the author of *The Odd Brain*.

HOW DID THAT GET UP THERE?

Be wary, dear reader, of leaving tubular objects sitting upright on the shower cubicle floor. 'Slipping over and falling backwards on to [insert name of offending object here]' appears to be the primary cause of mortally embarrassed people getting things jammed up their rectums and needing doctors to remove them.

What are the most frequently misplaced objects? The Wisconsin doctors, David Busch and James Starling, report the top ten in *Surgery* (1986, 100; 3: 512) after discovering 182 cases written up in the world's medical journals:

Object	Number removed
Glass or ceramic bottle or jar	32
Vibrator	23
Dildo	15
Glass or cup	12
Stick or broom handle	10
Light bulb	7
Tube	6
Carrot	4
Cucumber	3
Cattle horn	3

Mortifying shame can be the least of a victim's problems. Gordian Fulde, the emergency department director at St Vincent's Hospital, Darlinghurst, Australia, says getting rectum-jammed objects out is often far harder – and much more dangerous – than sticking them up there in the first place.

One German team only managed to remove a firmly lodged apple by mulching it with an argon laser, he says, while Athens doctors have resorted to using obstetric forceps to extract difficult objects. A rural Australian team used a suction plunger to pull out a glass bottle.

But one in ten cases still needs an operation, either to remove the object or to repair a perforated bowel. Such poor patients may end up with a colostomy, Fulde warns in the *Medical Journal of Australia* (1998, 169: 670).

FRACTURE OF THE PENIS

Beware of over-enthusiastic sex if you are aged fortysomething. Around one out of every 175,000 hospital admissions is for a fractured penis. Ouch.

It is caused when the erect penis is forcibly bent – in most cases during sexual intercourse. Dr Frederick Klein, the assistant professor of urology at the Medical College of Virginia in Richmond, explains. 'The patient hears a "crack" or "pop", and his penis immediately shrinks and then swells painfully and turns black and blue.'

The penis usually bends to the side opposite the injury; if the left corpus cavernosum is ruptured, for example, the penis will be bent to the right.

Dr Klein and colleagues report in the most appropriately named *Journal of Trauma* (1985, 25; 11: 1090) that patients are hospitalized for about two weeks on average, and good results are achieved in about 75 per cent of cases treated with surgery.

A global survey in the *British Journal of Surgery* (2002, 89; 5: 555) declared that penile fracture is 'not rare'. It found 1,331 cases were reported in medical journals between January 1935 and July 2001. Most reports were from the Mediterranean region. Most patients were aged in their forties.

FORGETTABLE SEX

Could intercourse ever be so good that you can't remember it? Japanese neuropsychiatrists at Tokushima University Medical School report how one of their woman patients had developed an alarming episode of complete amnesia after enjoying vigorous intercourse.

Sudden isolated bouts of complete memory loss and confusion in otherwise healthy people are called

transient global amnesia. Victims forget where they are and the identity of the people they are with. This can of course prove highly useful after a drunken one-night stand.

The Tokushima scientists report how sex caused the woman's amnesiac condition in the *Japanese Journal of Psychiatry and Neurology* (1993, 47; 1: 13). They speculate that it may be sparked by heightened blood pressure dropping rapidly after intercourse, causing a temporary fall in the brain's oxygen supply.

This might explain how the sufferers' ability to store new memories is also temporarily lost. The condition can also be caused by heavy exercise, particularly swimming in cold water. Attacks can last for several hours.

But in 1998, two blood specialists from America's Johns Hopkins University suggested in the *Lancet* (1998, 352; 9139: 1557) that the problem may be caused by tensing the abdominal muscles and straining, the way women do when giving birth – or having sex. This, they say, may cause a rush of blood to the brain – and it could affect one person in every ten thousand.

SOCCER-CUP CELIBACY

Bad news for football wives. The health-care market research company, Isis, claims that big sports events can ruin your love life.

It says a significant dip in prescriptions for erectile dysfunction drugs such as Viagra occurred during the World Cup in summer 2002 – a peak period for men sitting on the couch in front of the television with their pals and a bucket of cold beers.

The World Cup weeks saw the only drop in UK prescriptions over a two-year period: from around

25,000 a month, down to the 13,000 mark. Isis claims the two bouts of low-scoring are linked.

LARGE BUST OR BUST

If you are a woman with small breasts, you are also likely to be under-endowed in the intelligence department.

GP newspaper (15 December 2003) reports how a study by the University of Chicago has discovered that women with a breast size of D cup or greater score on average ten IQ points higher than those with an A or B cup.

But in fact having impressive frontal lobes does not necessarily mean a ticket to academic success, say the statisticians. They suggest that well-built women are in fact viewed as less intelligent because men pay more attention to their cleavage than to their conversation. Talk to the face, guys.

HISTORY'S TOP HYPOCHONDRIACS

I told you I was ill ...

One of the classic ironies of hypochondria is that you can spend so many years crying wolf that no one else worries when something really does go wrong.

Take the French playwright Molière, who used his lifetime's experience of health gripes to create Argon, the central character of his play, *The Imaginary Invalid*, always complaining about illness and fearing he was but a step away from the grave. Molière played the theatrical part himself – and sadly did it only too well. He died in 1672, on the evening of the satire's fourth performance, after suffering a coughing fit and haemorrhage on stage. His fellow actors had dismissed his earlier protestations of illness, so he had never got to see a doctor in time.

The American composer Leonard Bernstein met a similar fate. He spent 15 years in thrall to a variety of imaginary ailments. So when he started complaining of headaches, then suffered a blackout on stage and complained of smelling burning rubber, the doctors who checked him out were sceptical and said, ho hum, nothing seems to be wrong. After four days of hospital tests, they concluded he was suffering from a nervous affliction, probably self-induced. His medical form decreed, 'Most likely hysteria'.

His psychoanalyst also concluded that Bernstein's symptoms were all in the mind. One neurologist suggested he undergo a spinal tap, just to be sure there were no problems with his brain. But it is a painful procedure, and Bernstein would not go through with it. Five months later, and to everyone's surprise but Bernstein's, the composer fell into a coma. Several hours of surgery were to no avail. He had been suffering from a brain tumour and died in July 1990.

Should you wish to argue that hypochondria is a disease of the overactive imagination, then there is no shortage of artists, writers, actors, thinkers and megalomaniacs to back you up. Bernstein's fellow composer, Igor Stravinsky, was not only a hypochondriacal danger to himself. His family got caught up in his ill-health enthusiasms, too. Stravinsky went to see a doctor in every city he visited, and was also constantly swallowing pills that he prescribed for himself. In 1934, soon after his son, Theodore, needed emergency surgery for a ruptured appendix, Stravinsky had his own healthy appendix removed, 'as a precaution'. Cautious Igor ordered that the same operation be performed on his other three children, too.

Enrico Caruso was also the careful sort. The operatic tenor equipped himself with an armoury of atomizers, gargling fluids, migraine medicines and cold and cough cures wherever he travelled. He was also desperate to avoid catching skin complaints, so took his own linen with him to hotels. Before he occupied a suite it had to be sprayed with disinfectant. He would bathe and change his clothes after walking in the street or being in close contact with strangers in a public place. Before going to bed he saw that a mattress and piles of pillows were arranged around him on the floor lest he should fall out of bed in his sleep and hurt himself.

At least he had not been exposed to medical training. The father of evolutionary theory, Charles Darwin, began a lifetime of hypochondriacal suffering as a medical student, where many young people learn to imagine the horrors of encroaching illness. The British Medical Association nowadays warns proto-medics of this peril, but Darwin, as an evolutionist, would be pleased to know he was one of the first examples. He was a big man but a sensitive flower: 'It seems, as soon as the stimulus of mental work stops, my whole strength gives way,' he complained. Not only did he suffer from psychosomatic exhaustion, but Darwin also laboured with chronic intestinal disorders that seemed more in his mind than in his gut.

Psychoanalysts have had a jolly time suggesting that his stomach problems were rooted in the guilt he felt about toppling thousands of years of religious beliefs. But it wasn't all gloom and doom. Darwin liked sex – he married twice and produced several illegitimate children – and he prescribed sexual intercourse as a cure for hypochondria. At least it took his mind off things. A later scientific revolutionary, Sigmund Freud, would have agreed with this diagnosis: his simple explanation for hypochondria was that it is the product of the victim's libidinal energies being directed at their own body (in plain terms, the victim is screwing himself). It is not, he said, a matter for psychiatry.

But sex was a cause, rather than a cure, for the writer James Boswell's bodily obsessions. The 18th-century writer, the biographer of Johnson, was persistently haunted by the idea that he had contracted an incurable venereal disease. This may well have been sexual guilt. He had indeed caught a dose of VD as a youth, but the infection had cleared up. To distract himself from his syphilitic fixation, Boswell used to go out to watch public hangings. Better than sex, eh?

And Boswell always needed cheering up. He sank into his most severe hypochondria in 1763 when he went to study law at Utrecht University. 'A deep melancholy seized upon me. I groaned with the idea of living all winter in so shocking a place,' he complained in his journal. 'I was worse and worse the next day. All the horrid ideas you can imagine recurred upon me ... I sunk quite into despair. I thought at length the time was come that I should grow mad.' Boswell believed his affliction was hereditary. His mother, he said, was 'an extremely delicate girl, very hypochondriac'.

The poet Alfred Lord Tennyson, meanwhile, was fixated with the dread possibility of his eyesight failing. He worried about blindness his entire life. Ordinary floaters across his field of vision worried him. He called them 'animals', and wrote to his aunt, 'These animals you mention are very distressing and mine increase weekly; in fact I almost look forward with certainty to being blind some of these days.' Tennyson died in his eighties. His eyesight remained tolerably good.

That is another of the great ironies of hypochondria – so many of its sufferers go on to a ripe old age and achieve far more than the vast majority of people who feel happily healthy. Immanuel Kant, the metaphysical philosopher, wrote: 'Between health and insanity lies hypochondria,' and he was one to know.

The creator of the categorical imperative once claimed that his headaches were due to a special kind of electricity in the cloud systems. He also suspected that his organs were jammed together so tightly that they prevented him from breathing properly. Despite his lifetime of hypochondria, he never met with a serious illness, and died on 12 February 1804, at the ripe age of 79.

Florence Nightingale fought an even longer battle against her imagined illnesses on her way to lasting fame. Biographers speculate that it was her traumatic fight against death, disease and medical politics during the Crimean War that turned her into a sickness obsessive. In 1857, the year after she returned from the Crimea, she took to her bed, convinced that her life was in imminent danger.

Meanwhile, she continued to follow her vocation, to campaign for the establishment of nursing as a profession, and to set up London's Nightingale School for Nurses. She also pioneered the use of statistics in medicine. Her biographer, Lytton Strachey, wrote, 'She remained an invalid, but an invalid of curious character – an invalid who was too weak to walk downstairs and who worked harder than most cabinet ministers … her illness, whatever it may have been, was not inconvenient.' Like all hypochondriacs, she was proved right in the end – though she had to wait until 1910, when she was 90 years old, before death caught up with her.

History's other celebrity homebound achiever, Marcel Proust, made a literary career from novels peopled with sickness and morbid psychology. There can be few better examples of that ancient piece of literary advice: write about what you know. 'Infirmity alone makes us take notice and learn, and enables us to analyse processes which we would otherwise know nothing about,' wrote Proust, and he certainly knew a lot about infirmity.

Proust had a 'severely troubled' stomach and reportedly ate only once a day from a select group of foods. He experienced terrible insomnia at night and spent his life as a perpetual invalid, passing through a succession of colds and fevers. He stayed indoors as much as possible because he was terrified of germs – and even refused to open windows. He also thought that he was allergic to strong light, and said his skin was so sensitive he could not use soap – so he avoided baths and preferred instead to dab himself with a collection of damp towels. Noise from neighbours drove him nearly mad – which is bad news if you stay in all day – hence his life in a cork-lined sound-insulated room.

In his novel sequence *Remembrance of Things Past*, Proust wrote, 'For each illness that doctors cure with medicine, they provoke it in ten healthy people by inoculating them with the virus that is a thousand times more powerful than any microbe: the idea that one is ill.' Fortunately for hypochondriac posterity, our Frenchman completed all seven volumes of *Remembrance of Things Past* before he contracted pneumonia and died at the age of 51.

But you don't have to start out as an effetely nervous wreck to end up a hypochondriacal recluse. How about beginning as an oil tycoon, record-breaking daredevil pilot, political intriguer, movie mogul and the man once nicknamed the 'world's greatest womanizer'?

That would be Howard Hughes, who started his career as an oil-millionaire playboy and ended it as an emaciated hermit. Things began to go wrong for

Hughes when he was severely injured in a serious air crash in 1946 and subsequently became addicted to morphine. Later he moved to Las Vegas and began increasingly to shun society as a severe hypochondriacal fear of infection took hold. In his 18 years of seclusion he had a huge air purifier installed into a car that took up most of the boot and cost more than the limousine itself.

Up in the hotel he owned, he had his food delivered in paper bags that had previously remained untouched in a sealed cupboard for two years. The drivers had to wear white cotton hospital gloves when they carried the bags. Hughes extracted the food – mostly Hershey bars and milk – with Kleenex wrapped around his hand.

He had strict rules over the delivery of magazines. Three copies of the same magazine were always presented to him. Hughes would reach out, his hands and arms swathed in paper, and delicately remove the middle magazine from its companions. He would repeat, over and over again, instructions for the other magazines to be burned. He also used a minimum of 15 tissues to open his cabinets. His last political cause was to try to stop underground nuclear testing in Nevada, because he was so terrified of radiation.

Is capitalism in itself a cause of hypochondria? Not if you are Nicolae Ceaucescu. When the Communist dictator of Romania visited a Transylvanian castle early in his rule, it was not the prospect of vampires that rattled him. His guide around Peles Castle, a fine German Renaissance building and one of Romania's national treasures, was rash enough to point out that some of the castle woodwork was afflicted by fungus.

The fungus was no danger to humans, but Ceaucescu had a morbid fear of infections, and left the place there and then, never to return. There was a bright side – Ceaucescu's paranoia meant he left the area well alone – never subjecting it to the brutalist concrete modernization that wrecked places such as Bucharest.

Ceaucescu was not the only megalomaniac to have given hypochondriacs a bad name. He pales in comparison with Adolf Hitler, both in despotism and health paranoia. In fact, Hitler has a strong claim to being history's greatest hypochondriac. To begin with the mundane items, he constantly fretted about his health, was fanatical about cleanliness, never drank alcohol, never smoked and never allowed anyone to smoke in his presence.

When he learnt that he had shaken hands with a former prostitute who was marrying one of his generals, he immediately took multiple showers. His hyper-ambitious deputy Martin Bormann managed to have one of Hitler's closest friends, Heinrich Hoffmann, banned from Hitler's company. Knowing about Hitler's hypochondria, Bormann scurrilously informed him that Hoffmann was carrying a contagious disease. A distressed Hitler refused to have Hoffmann come anywhere near him.

There were other worries, too. Hitler's mother had died of cancer and Adolf desperately feared he would be stricken with the disease as well. His fear intensified when he had surgery to remove a polyp from his throat. Even though he was reassured by doctors that the polyp was benign, he was convinced that it was cancer. He wrote his last will and testament in 1938, certain that he was going to die before he completed his political plans.

Hitler became even more obsessed with his health after the failed assassination attempt on him in 1944. His doctor prescribed drugs of his own design that contained hemlock. Hitler gulped so many pills he was slowly poisoning himself. Tremors in his right hand became acute, and he rarely allowed photographs or film of him after July 1944.

But the dictator did not just keep his hypochondria to himself. He tried to instil it into an entire country. One of his party's slogans instructed the German people: 'Your body belongs to the nation! Your body belongs to the Führer! You have the duty to be healthy! Food is not a private matter.'

Hitler's exhortations are reminiscent of the new brand of healthy-eating message that Western governments increasingly use to imply that being overweight is not only unhealthy, but an irresponsible burden on the state's meagre health and welfare resources. Body fascism? Health Nazism? Could it all be the product of power-crazed politicians' contagious hypochondria?

EAT, DRINK AND ...

Be merry, for tomorrow you may worry yourself dead

MISFORTUNE COOKIES

The trouble with Chinese food, the old saying goes, is that after you've had one meal, you get hungry and want another one. Not if you suffer from **Chinese restaurant syndrome**.

The symptoms, identified in 1968 by Dr Robert Byck, a Yale Medical School psychiatrist and brain researcher, are headache, sweats and hot flushes, chest pain, numbness or burning in and around the mouth, and a sense of facial pressure or swelling. Medical tests show victims have abnormal heart rhythm, rapid heart rate and restricted breathing.

Most people recover from mild cases of Chinese restaurant syndrome on their own. But some researchers claim it can be life-threatening, with all the symptoms of severe anaphylactic shock reaction, such as throat-swelling.

Why would an innocent sweet-and-sour wreak such havoc? The *New York Times* (21 August 1999) reports that Byck blamed the flavour enhancer monosodium glutamate (MSG) for sparking reactions in susceptible people. He did his research in a restaurant near his lab and his findings led to MSG being banned from American baby food. But the claims have sparked widely conflicting reports from research studies, with many arguing that the link is not proven.

Monosodium glutamate is chemically similar to one of the brain's neurotransmitters, glutamate, and the anti-MSG camp claims this is significant. The additive is also blamed for **glutamate-induced asthma** and, less obviously, **hot dog headache**, by chemotherapy experts at Mount Sinai Medical Center, New York, in *Medical Hypotheses* (1992, 38; 3: 185). While the link remains unproved, foodsellers will continue to pep up their dishes with MSG.

Hot dogs should carry a health warning anyway, according to John Peters, a University of Southern California epidemiologist who claims in the journal *Cancer Causes and Control* (1994, 5; 2: 195) that children who eat more than 12 hot dogs a month appear to have nine times the normal risk of developing childhood leukaemia. As well as **hot dog-related leukaemia**, the journal also reports that children born to fathers who ate hot dogs before conception have a significantly increased risk of developing brain tumours.

CHICKEN OUCH MEIN

Headaches and possible death are not the only threats you face when going for a Chinese meal. Using chopsticks may cause arthritis.

A study of more than 2,500 residents of Beijing found that osteoarthritis is more common in the hands used to operate chopsticks, and specifically the thumb and the second and third joints on the first and third fingers which are stressed by chopstick use, researchers report in *Arthritis and Rheumatology* (2004, 50; 5: 1495).

Dr David Hunter of the Boston University School of Medicine and colleagues interviewed 2,507 60-year-old residents in randomly selected Beijing neighbour-hoods. 'This study suggests that chopsticks may play a role in the development of hand osteoarthritis,' Hunter says. 'We recommend further biomechanical research to evaluate the forces involved in chopstick use.'

SAUSAGE SCARE

Eating blood sausage before undergoing a cancer test could result in your having unnecessary hospital pro-cedures.

Stomach surgeons gathered volunteers from the Lancashire town of Bury, known as the black-pudding capital of the world, and asked them to eat the local sausage delicacy, which is made from congealed pigs' blood.

The research team, from Frenchay Hospital, Bris-tol, discovered that black pudding can produce false positive results in screening tests for cancers of the colon and rectum. The tests look for blood in people's stools, and can't tell the difference between pigs' blood and human blood, says the report in the *British Medical Journal* (2002, 325; 7378: 1444).

The doctors then surveyed 100 people about their eating habits and discovered some 63 per cent of them occasionally succumb to the temptation of a sausage full of pig plasma. This led them to conclude that, thanks to black puddings, more than twice the expected number of people may test positive for colon and rectal cancer – and be sent to hospital for needless further investigations.

DRINKING FOR STONERS

Cutting your alcohol intake is most likely a good thing. But sobriety could increase women's chances of developing gallstones. Females who like a drink or three are less likely to develop gallstone problems, say researchers from the Harvard School of Public Health. It is not only inhibitions that are soluble in alcohol: the booze seems to hinder the stones' development.

The researchers studied more than 80,000 nurses to discover the link, which they report in the *American Journal of Clinical Nutrition* (2003, 78; 2: 339). And it doesn't matter what type of alcohol you drink.

The authors suggest, in obligatory killjoy mode, however, that, 'Despite the inverse association between regular, moderate alcohol intake and gallstone disease, interested patients should discuss the health effects of alcohol consumption with their healthcare providers, who can help determine the patients' overall health risks and benefits, as well as provide an individual clinical recommendation.'

BETTER FROM THE BOTTLE ...

That bottle-sucking wino could be drinking more safely than you. Italian researchers say you can get dangerous amounts of lead in your bloodstream by drinking from shiny new lead crystal glasses. But it depends on what you drink out of them. Cola drinks are safe because they draw very little lead from the glass. But who drinks cola out of crystalware?

White wine, which you are far more likely to quaff from crystal glasses, draws the highest level of lead of any of the liquids studied, reports the journal *Food Additives and Contamination* (2000, 17; 3: 205).

Once you start washing your glasses, however, the rules change. When a crystal glass has been through the dishwasher three times, the level of lead in wine stays the same, but the level of lead in the cola drinks increases, say researchers at the glass study institute Stazione Sperimentale del Vetro of Murano-Venezia, Italy.

SOFT TAP HEART ATTACKS

Health promoters are forever badgering us to drink more water. But health scares involving costly bottled products – Perrier was once found to be contaminated with benzene, and Coke's UK brand has recently been discovered to contain excess levels of a suspected carcinogen – might prompt you to guzzle gallons of tap water instead. That might not work either – your house supply could be boosting your risk of a heart attack, a study claims.

People who live in areas with soft tap water have significantly increased risk of cardiac death compared with their hard-water counterparts, say researchers in Finland. They studied 19,000 men aged between 35 and 74 who had suffered heart attacks, and found that for every unit increase in water softness there is a 1 per cent increase in the risk of coronary failure.

The researchers claim in the *Journal of Epidemiology and Community Health* (2004, 58; 2: 136) that the findings explain regional variations in heart attack rates of up to 40 per cent. They examined the minerals dissolved in hard water, and suggest that higher fluoride levels in it may help protect heart function.

But not all hard water is good news. For every microgram of dissolved iron per litre in some types of hard water, the heart risk increases by an average of 4 per cent, the epidemiologists say, and for every microgram of copper per litre of water, it increases by 10 per cent.

CUPPAHOLICS ANONYMOUS

Alcohol, as we all know, can drive you into the arms of strangeness. But tea and coffee can have the same effect – if you fall victim to **caffeinism**.

Some medical experts believe caffeinism is similar to alcoholism in that sufferers are the last to realize they have a problem. Symptoms can include confusion, restlessness, nervousness, insomnia, sweating and palpitations. In extreme cases, manic behaviour and panic disorders can develop. In one recorded case, a soldier serving in the Indian Army was believed to have been blinded by drinking too much tea.

The condition last came to light in 1997 as part of the defence case of a senior British Army officer accused of false accounting. Major David Senior, a decorated helicopter pilot in the Army Air Corps, had drunk up to a gallon of tea every day for 20 years of his life.

Charles Gabb, defending, told Major Senior's court martial hearing: 'On first hearing this, some people may laugh but he was known as a teetotaller who drank an enormous quantity of tea.' He said his client had not been dishonest in any way but may have made a genuine mistake with paperwork relating to the funds because of his condition.

The *Daily Mail* (13 June 1997) reports that all the charges of false accounting and theft against him were dropped.

CRASH DIET? HERE ARE THE SCARS

Obesity is currently touted as a massive health threat, but if you try a tough diet, you may run the risk of harming your looks. The American Academy of Cosmetic Surgeons issued the warning after discovering that vegetarians on poorly balanced food intakes suffer scarring and delayed healing after relatively superficial operations.

The Academy says weight-conscious eaters are at significantly increased risk of scarring if they restrict their diets to cut out wound-healing nutrients. It says in the *Journal of the American Medical Association* (1995, 273; 12: 910) that these include albumin, which is found in proteins, glucose from carbohydrates, essential fatty acids, vitamins A, C, K and B-complex, and the minerals zinc, copper, iron and manganese.

SLIM HEALTH CHANCES

But if you are slim, you may have no reason to scoff. Losing weight may not be the great health-enhancer anyway. It might not be fatness, but fitness that counts, say doctors who warn that thin couch potatoes are at more risk of illness than fat people who exercise.

Unfit men who are not obese have almost three times the death rate of other men who are fit but medically obese, say researchers at the Cooper Institute for Aerobics Research in Dallas, Texas, which studied 25,000 males for nearly 20 years.

The institute's director of research, Steven Blair, told a London conference in July 1997 that when researchers normally study obese people, they discover illnesses that they blame on fat. In fact it is their laziness that's unhealthy, he claimed at the Health Education Authority conference.

WHO ORDERED THE HAEMORRHAGE?

Gourmet food – all those exorbitantly priced exotic dishes comprising bits of endangered species swimming in rich fatty sauces – are as much a threat to your finances as they are to your arteries. But you could become obsessed with the stuff if you suffer a reasonably common form of brain haemorrhage.

Researchers cite the case of a patient who suffered a haemorrhage and became so obsessed with rich food that eating soon became the only conversational topic that interested him. In his daily diary, he recorded yearnings for bespoke sausage and mash or escalopes of game in cream sauce. The 48-year-old journalist had had no previous interest in food – but when he returned to work after recovering from his haemorrhage, he started writing about exotic food.

Another haemorrhage patient experienced a similar foodie preoccupation, which prompted the doctors to start a three-year study. They found that, of more than 700 brain-haemorrhage patients, 36 developed what they named **gourmand syndrome**. They say in *Neurology* (1997, 48; 5: 1185) that brain damage can sometimes unlock distant memories or unleash inhibitions, and it is possible that in some it revives a buried passion for food.

BUDDING DISASTER

Is your tongue about to get you into trouble? We all have different concentrations of tastebuds on our tongues, and a quarter of us are so-called 'super-tasters', with highly sensitive palates.

This may sound great, but it can be to your peril, warn scientists at Wayne State University in America. Supertasters inhabit a 'neon taste world' in which sensations such as bitterness are magnified. And this may put them off green vegetables such as broccoli, and similar foods known to help protect against cancer. Dr Linda Bartoshuk studied a group of men's colon-cancer screening results and found a link between the number of precancerous colon polyps and the men's taste sensitivity.

There is some good news, though. Supertasters seem to have lower risk of heart disease, according to work by Dr Bartoshuk's colleague, Valerie Duffy. She suggests that this is probably because they tend not to like sweet and fatty foods, in the *Journal of the American Dietetics Association* (2000, 100; 6: 647).

SALT AND BATTERY

Look out for those tiny batteries that come in watches, cameras and telephones. In fact look out for the bigger ones, too. There seems to be a strange human compulsion to swallow them.

Georgetown University's National Capital Poison Center has reported 2,382 cases of adults and children swallowing batteries over a seven-year period in the journal *Pediatrics* (1992, 89: 747–757). Most of them were button-sized batteries used in hearing aids and watches, but there were also much larger cylindrical cells.

The Center says that a surprisingly high number of adult patients have mistaken the batteries for pills. 'One guy was walking down the street, reached into his pocket for something for a headache, and popped a battery in his mouth,' says Georgetown's Dr Toby Litovitz, the author of the study.

Another patient was taking a heart pill and changing her hearing-aid battery at the same time and mixed the two up. 'She didn't realize what had happened until her hearing aid didn't work.' She couldn't have heard her heart beating either, which must have been doubly distressing.

It takes 48 hours for a battery to pass through the intestinal tract. The battery usually corrodes, leaking its alkaline fluids into the body. The poisons are often so diluted by body fluids that they cause little harm, though one in ten patients suffered symptoms such as vomiting and nausea.

The chief danger, says Dr Litovitz, is that the button batteries can become lodged in the oesophagus and have to be removed surgically. All six of the larger batteries, most of them size AAA, passed through the swallowers' bodies safely.

POISONOUS PECKERS

Having your morning milk bottles pecked by birds is more than just a pesky irritant, it could cause you serious food poisoning, says a public-health expert.

Carol Phillips, of Nene College, Northampton, says the bacteria *Camphylobacter* spp. are one of the most common causes of food-borne illness in the UK, and she has blamed birds that peck through bottle and carton tops as a significant cause.

She videotaped doorsteps of a small group of houses in Northamptonshire where morning milk deliveries were being pecked by magpies, crows, sparrows, tits and blackbirds. Then she tested the birds for camphylobacter infection. The magpies and crows proved positive for the bacteria, as did the milk they pecked.

'Drinking milk from bottles attacked by birds is a potential health risk,' she writes in the *Lancet* (1995, 346; 8971: 386), adding that seasonal bird attacks on milk could well explain seasonal rises in camphylobacter infection in humans.

CHRIST'S BLOODY PERIL

Communion is at the heart of Christian fellowship, but that doesn't mean it is absolved from the normal rules of hygiene: so churchgoers should beware of poisoned chalices. Bernard Hudson, the head of microbiology and infectious diseases at Royal North Shore Hospital, Sydney, has warned the city's Anglicans to use individual cups to cut the infection risk.

The *Medical Post* (15 April 2003) says a report by the doctor dispels the notion that the wine in the chalice, which symbolizes Christ's blood, kills any infection. And, he adds, 'It is not true to state that wiping the communion cup reduces the amount of infectious agent present to a level lower than the infectious dose.'

Hudson has told the church it could be held liable if a parishioner contracts a disease such as the cold sore virus or meningococcal septicemia from sharing saliva. He says, too, that dispensing bread with unwashed hands could spread diarrhoea. And even churches can't get insurance cover for acts of God.

PASSOVER PASS-OUT

The locusts, boils, and even the angel of death have passed over, but if you are an observant Jew, you now face a new threat to your children – from Passover lamps. A study of New Yorkers has discovered how Jewish toddlers risk poisoning from the lamp oil that illuminates holy days.

Dr Robert J. Hoffman of Manhattan's Beth Israel Medical Center had noticed that on many Fridays when he worked at the city's Poison Control Center, urgent calls came in about children who had swallowed paraffin oil. 'It turned out they were Jewish,' Hoffman says. The accidents often happened during the Sabbath, from sunset on Friday until sunset on Saturday, or on Jewish holidays such as Passover.

The oil can cause coughing, vomiting and inflammation of the lungs. Hoffman found the cases shared a similar cause: 'The lamps have a metal tube that serves as a wick. And when the lamp is not lit, the tube looks like a perfect straw to a child,' he says.

The risk of paraffin-oil poisoning among the city's Orthodox children is about 370 times higher than in the general population, warns Hoffman's study in *Pediatrics* (2004, 113; 4: e377). He says that from 2000 to

2003 in New York, 32 out of 45 oil-poisoning cases involved Orthodox Jewish children whose average age was under two.

LOW-CHOLESTEROL KILLERS?

So, you have paid heed to all the health warnings and cut your cholesterol intake. That may well have strongly reduced your chances of premature demise through heart attack, stroke or high blood pressure. But it seems you may also have somewhat boosted your chances of dying by your own hand – or by someone else's.

The cholesterol debate is not as one-sided as you might think. Large-scale health-promotion initiatives have shown that reducing cholesterol consumption reduces your chance of dying from cardiovascular disease, but a report in the British Medical Journal (1994, 309; 6942: 421) says that if you cut your cholesterol intake it could increase your chances of death through fatal accidents, suicide and violence.

This has sparked controversy among researchers, who deny such studies' conclusions are valid. But several explanations have been proposed for the strange phenomenon. A University of California study in the Lancet (1993, 341; 8837: 75) reports a link between low cholesterol and increased incidence of depression among men aged over 70. It suggests that this may be because low cholesterol levels shorten the amount of time the feelgood hormone serotonin is effective in the brain.

Some studies on mice show that cholesterol might help the central nervous system to suppress harmful behavioural impulses, while monkeys in zoos have been found to become abnormally aggressive when put on low-fat diets, according to a report in *Psychosomatic Medicine* (1991, 53; 6: 634), though maybe they simply took offence at having their butter swapped for margarine.

Men who murder in a fit of rage have also been found to show below-average cholesterol levels. A study in the *Lancet* (1992, 340; 8826: 995) suggests that some cholesterol-reducing drugs may increase aggressive behaviour as a side-effect, thus increasing patients' chances of getting into trouble.

But the criminal behaviour seems to happen regardless of medication. University of California, Los Angeles, medical researchers compared the blood-cholesterol tests of 79,777 Swedes with their subsequent police records. They found that lower than average cholesterol was strongly associated with criminal violence, even when the criminals were compared with people the same age and sex, who had the same levels of education and drinking patterns, says a report in the *Journal of Psychiatric Research* (2000, 34; 4–5: 301).

KARAOKE VICTIMS

Saloon-bar researchers have confirmed what many already suspect: karaoke singing can damage your health. Strenuous singing can injure the voice and increase the risk of deafness, according to two studies.

Researchers in Korea measured sound-pressure levels during ballads and rock. They also measured each singer's hearing threshold levels before and after

100 minutes of karaoke. Results showed that noise levels frequently exceeded the US Occupational Safety and Health Administration's limit of 115 decibels, roughly equivalent to having a pneumatic drill going a metre away from your head – only it doesn't sound as good.

'Up to 8dB of significant hearing loss was found at the most important human hearing frequency band after about two hours of karaoke. It may pose a serious threat,' warns the study, in the *International Journal of Industrial Ergonomics* (2003, 31: 375–385).

In a second study, Hong Kong University researchers warn in the *Journal of Voice* (2003, 17: 216–227) that the singers who do it 'my way' risk committing vocal kamikaze. 'As most of the karaoke singers have no formal training in singing, these amateur singers are more vulnerable to developing voice problems under these intensive singing activities,' they discovered.

If you really want to trash your voice, hit the booze, avoid water and go crazy. 'Subjects who sang continuously without drinking water and taking rests showed significant changes in the jitter measure [i.e. warbling] and the highest pitch they could produce during singing,' the researchers conclude.

SID VICIOUS SYNDROME

Harvard doctor Robert Caspari is no fan of punk rock. He reports in the *New England Journal of Medicine* (1980, 303; 24: 1420) how it can ruin your eyesight.

His patient, a healthy 20-year-old man with a youthful taste in loud music, arrived at the surgery complaining of redness in both eyes that had persisted for four days. On examination, Dr Caspari found haemorrhaging in both eyes, but no immediate cause.

'After close questioning, the patient disclosed that on the night before the appearance of the redness he had been vigorously involved in a dance called the "pogo" which is performed to New Wave music,' says the doctor. 'Reportedly this requires repeated bouncing movements for long periods of time.'

DANCEFLOOR DISEASE

Johns Hopkins Hospital doctors have identified a scourge of rhythm-crazy teens: **disco felon**. They write in the *New England Journal of Medicine* (1979, 301; 3: 166) how they discovered it when treating a 17-year-old girl with an abscess on her middle finger. On close questioning, she said it had been caused by an infected crack in the skin – and the crack had been caused by constantly clicking her fingers in time to the music.

DISC DIGIT

Another recreational disease to afflict the middle digit is **Frisbee finger**. This emerged in the mid-seventies at the start of the Frisbee craze. Doctor Halley Faust of Philadelphia points out that the problem of infected finger cuts is greater among urban Frisbee throwers because the disc lands on hard surfaces, which makes the edges jagged. 'The syndrome does occur if you overdo it with smooth-edged Frisbees as well, however, and should not be ruled out in subjects from more rural settings,' he points out in the *New England Journal of Medicine* (1975, 293; 14: 725).

✚

HAVE YOU GOT THE BIG H?

Worried about being excessively worried about your health?

One classic definition of hypochondria is that it is 'an irrational fear of disease so great that it disrupts normal living'. Of course, that is clinically serious hypochondria rather than the lifestyle-level of daily health obsession we are nowadays all encouraged to feel. But you can find out your fear-factor by trying this Whitely Index questionnaire.

The Whiteley Index is the standard self-test for hypochondria. For each question, circle the number that best describes how you feel.

1 = Not at all
2 = A little
3 = Moderately
4 = Quite a bit
5 = A great deal

1. Do you worry a lot about your health?
    1 2 3 4 5

2. Do you think there is something seriously wrong with your body?
    1 2 3 4 5

3. Is it hard for you to forget about yourself and to think about all sorts of other things?
   1 2 3 4 5

4. If you feel ill and someone tells you that you are looking better, do you become annoyed?
   1 2 3 4 5

5. Do you find that you are often aware of various things happening in your body?
   1 2 3 4 5

6. Are you bothered by many aches and pains?
   1 2 3 4 5

7. Are you afraid of illness?
   1 2 3 4 5

8. Do you worry about your health more than most people?
   1 2 3 4 5

9. Do you get the feeling that people are not taking your illnesses seriously?
   1 2 3 4 5

10. Is it hard for you to believe your doctor when he tells you there is nothing to worry about?
    1 2 3 4 5

11. Do you often worry about the possibility that you have a serious illness?
    1 2 3 4 5

12. If a disease is brought to your attention (through radio, TV or newspapers, or someone you know), do you worry about getting it yourself?
1 2 3 4 5

13. Do you find that you are bothered by many different symptoms?
1 2 3 4 5

14. Do you often have the symptoms of a very serious illness?
1 2 3 4 5

Add up the circled numbers. The higher your total, the higher your chances of being excessively worried about your health. There are no definite parameters in the Whiteley Index, but if you score between 32 and 55 (or even more than that) you are generally considered a hypochondriac. If you score between 14 and 28, you are generally thought normal. These numbers are merely indications, however, and people suffering from depression can also often score high.

Even if you don't score highly, though, you were concerned enough to complete the questionnaire – which must say something. The rampant popularity of questionnaires in modern media is in itself a symptom of our hypo-maniac society. Magazine readers in particular are mugs for quick self-test diagnoses for trivially devastating afflictions: Are you a sex addict? Do you suffer low self-esteem? What's your neurosis rating? Check your gullibility quotient! Are you addicted to questionnaires?

DOCTORS' DISTRACTION

Joining the medical profession does not help to protect you from this crawling malaise. It makes it worse. Oliver Howes, a psychiatrist at the Maudsley Hospital, London, warns in the *Lancet* (1998, 351; 9112: 1332) that some studies have found that about 70 per cent of medical students have been found to suffer occasional bouts of hypochondriasis – which is medically defined as a 'persistent, unrealistic preoccupation with the possibility of having a serious disease', and where 'common, normal sensations and appearances are often misinterpreted as abnormal and signs of disease'.

Among the junior medics it is known as **medical studentitis** and their health worries are often linked to the illness they happen to be studying at the time. Howes adds that other professions reportedly prone to hypochondria are actors and musicians. Writers, politicians and business types appear particularly high-risk too.

HYPOCHONDRIA – THE SYMPTOMS

Dr F.E. Kenyon, a British psychiatrist who has spent most of his professional life working with hypochondriacs, says in the *British Journal of Psychiatry* (1976, 1; 29: 1) that the most common places for imagined pains are the head and neck, followed by the abdomen and then the chest.

Head and neck complaints include dizziness, hearing one's own pulse at night, loss of hearing, a lump in the throat, throat clearing or cough, and floaters that drift across one's field of vision. Gastrointestinal complaints include indigestion in all its forms, followed by pains and bowel disorders.

Kenyon adds that chest complaints most usually concern palpitations, skipped heartbeats, pain on one side, racing pulse, inability to take a deep breath, involuntary sighing and a sense of increased blood pressure. And from which side of the body do the mysterious pains emanate? Kenyon says that, inexplicably, around 70 per cent of complaints are on the left.

CLINIC CAPERS

If the illness doesn't get you,
the medics will

NOVICE ALERT

Try not to get hospitalized in the first week in August in Britain, says Dr Paul Siklos, a consultant physician at West Suffolk Hospital.

He sparked controversy in the *British Medical Journal* (1995, 310; 6979: 597) by claiming that an influx of newly qualified house officers may be linked to an increase of deaths in hospitals. The previous week may be no better, he says: that is the week when junior medical staff flock to take annual leave before the new influx.

WEEKEND WIPEOUT

If you are planning an emergency hospitalization, avoid weekends. Patients admitted to surgical intensive care units on Saturday or Sunday are 30 per cent more likely to die than those admitted on weekdays, researchers from a large teaching hospital have found. You need not worry, however, if it is a medical or multi-speciality intensive care unit, because they don't seem to suffer the weekend dip.

'We don't really know why surgical patients admitted on the weekend didn't fare as well,' says Dr Allen Ensminger, of the Mayo Clinic Minnesota. 'Potentially there is a delay in seeking a surgeon for the patient admitted on the weekend,' he told an

American Thoracic Society International Conference. Perhaps weekends are a good time to have a heart attack on the golf course instead.

CHRISTMAS CORONARY

Christmas seems a bad time, too. Heart-attack patients admitted to American hospitals during the winter holidays have higher mortality rates than those admitted during the rest of the year. Experts from Duke University Medical Center studied 134,000 medical records and found that during the holiday period patients are more likely to receive second-rate drugs or surgery.

Why? It appears that the best doctors and surgeons have made sure that they get time off to spend with their families, leaving people unfortunate enough to get coronaries for Christmas in the hands of less able staff, says evidence presented to the American College of Cardiology.

OUT-OF-HOURS EVIL

Try to avoid having heart surgery out of normal office hours. Coronary angioplasty is twice as likely to fail on heart-attack patients if performed before 8 a.m. and after 6 p.m.

The Dutch findings, in the *Journal of the American College of Cardiology* (2003, 41; 12: 2138), suggest that the body's circadian rhythms have a strong impact on how well patients survive angioplasty operations. However, the results also raise concern that the surgery results are worse for patients who have operations outside normal duty hours. So is it bodily rhythms at fault, or the fact that doctors don't like working anti-social hours?

In the same issue of the journal, doctors at the University of Massachusetts Medical School in Worcester say there is strong evidence that sleep deprivation impairs doctors' cognitive performance and motor function (i.e. it makes them dozy and clumsy). This could mean some rather cack-handed medical care at night.

THREE MINUTES – NO, TWO MINUTES – TO LIVE

Doctors may be able to predict times when they are not up to the job, but their colleagues who try to predict your death are seldom right. Researchers in the *British Medical Journal* (2003, 327; 7408: 195) compared doctors' predictions of how long dying patients had to live with the length of time they actually did live, in eight studies involving 1563 people.

The doctors, perhaps surprisingly, proved to be optimists. Maybe they have too much faith in their handiwork. While the medics predicted on average that patients had 42 days to live, the average survival was only 29 days. And although in a quarter of cases they were correct within seven days, more often than that they were out by at least four weeks.

The researchers, from Australia's Royal Prince Alfred Hospital in Camperdown, suggest that on average, doctors overestimate people's remaining life span by 30 per cent. So if the doctor does announce that you have only three minutes to live, don't bother trying to boil an egg.

BODY TALK, A+E STYLE

Want fast treatment in accident and emergency? Don't cross your legs, suggest Micha Rapoport and colleagues at the Assaf Harofeb Medical Centre, Zerifin, Israel, in the *Lancet* (1995, 345; 8956: 1060).

They say their experience of working in the emergency rooms has taught them that when patients arrive on a stretcher with any of their limbs crossed – such as crossed ankles, crossed hands behind the neck, or hands folded across the stomach – 'they are highly unlikely to have any acute condition, leaving ample time for tests and observation'. Keep your legs apart – you'll get seen quicker.

HOSPITAL – THE WORST PLACE TO BE ILL

One of the greatest dangers of being a hypochondriac is the fact that sooner or later some helpful medic is bound to believe there may be something genuinely physically wrong with you. Then they send you for medical investigations and perhaps even an operation. But watch out, there are bodgers about, says a report in the *Journal of the American Medical Association* (2003, 290; 14: 1868) as shown below.

Hazards of hospitalization:

- *Serious blood infection after surgery: 22 per cent of patients who contracted this died*
- *Rupture of a wound after surgery: nearly 10 per cent died of the injury*
- *Infections caused by medical care: this killed 4 per cent of patients who contracted one*

Medical injuries in hospitals claim more than 32,500 lives in the United States each year, according to the study of hospital-care complications, led by Dr Chunliu Zhan, of the Agency for Healthcare Research and Quality, who spent two years identifying medical injuries in 7.5 million hospital cases from 2000. Dr Zhan says that the safest procedure in hospital is the delivery of a baby naturally, without the help of instruments. 'Not too many people would die from those injuries.'

Zhan's figures may, however, be a rather conservative estimate. *Effective Clinical Practice* (2000, 3; 6: 277) says a report by the American Institute of Medicine on medical errors concludes that around 3.3 per cent of hospital admissions result in a fatal error, and that half of these – between 44,000 and 98,000 patient deaths each year – are preventable. That would mean that up to 268 people in America a day – equivalent to an airliner-load – are dying unnecessarily, thanks to doctors' mistakes.

PRESCRIPTION PERILS

It is not only the medics who could get you. Prescribed drugs wreak their own havoc. In Australia, an estimated 6 per cent of all hospital admissions and some 800 deaths a year are caused by people taking their medication wrongly, reports the *Australian Health Review* (1998, 21; 4: 260). We fret continually about the prospect of young people having access to recreational drugs, but rarely seem worried about telling confused and ill people to take jars of potentially lethal chemicals home with them.

OOPS, NOW WHERE'S THAT CLAMP?

Most popular places in the body for surgeons to leave instruments inside you after operations:

- *Abdomen or pelvis: 54 per cent*
- *Vagina: 22 per cent*
- *Chest: 7.4 per cent*
- *Others such as spinal canal, face, brain and extremities: 17 per cent*

You are most at risk if you have emergency surgery or an unexpected change in your operation. In that case, the odds are between four and nine times greater that the surgeons will leave something untoward inside your body. Your risk also rises significantly if you are overweight: hefty people are more likely to have objects left inside them because there is more room to lose things.

Sponges or instruments are left behind at least 1,500 times a year in the United States, say researchers led by Dr Atul Gawande, a surgeon at Brigham and Women's Hospital in Boston. They say leaving objects behind is 'an uncommon but dangerous error' that can lead to severe infections, organ damage and sometimes even death.

In some cases surgical sponges (which are actually gauze pads) left in patients become embedded in tissue and are mistaken for tumours. As a result, patients have had parts of their intestines removed. Such errors occur in one out of every 9,000 to 19,000 operations where the body cavity is opened – about one case a year for a typical large hospital, says the report in the *New England Journal of Medicine* (2003, 348; 3: 229).

In the language of medical journals, surgical tools sewn up inside people are not lost, forgotten or left behind; rather, they are 'retained'. 'It is kind of a euphemism,' Gawande says. 'It implies a certain lack of responsibility, or that the instrument did it itself.'

The profession has coined a word for a left-behind surgical sponge: **gossypiboma**, from the Latin word *gossypium* for cotton and the Swahili *boma* for 'place of concealment'.

HOUSE-BRICK HYMEN

It is not only medics who leave things in inappropriate cavities. Doctors in the *Journal of the Indian Medical Association* (2002, 100; 11: 671) report the case of a 60-year-old woman who turned up at hospital reporting constipation and pain in the lower abdomen. A rectal examination found a strange mass obstructing her bowel. Careful manipulation removed the object from her vagina. It measured 15cm × 12cm × 12cm, and was a house brick. The patient said it helped with her prolapse.

WHITE COAT CHAOS

Professional incompetence is not the only medical threat to us patients. Simply wearing doctors' clothes can be a danger. It is called the **white coat effect**. People who get panicked by health professionals give out strange diagnostic results, as shown by Toronto University researchers who compared blood pressure readings taken by doctors in surgery with those taken by civilians outside hospital.

They report in the *American Journal of Hypertension* (2003, 16; 6: 494) that the average readings taken by civilians were significantly lower than the doctors' –

155mmHg compared to 174mmHg. Such a disparity can mean the difference between 'normal' and 'troublesome'.

But people whose blood pressure is liable to be sent soaring by the white-coat effect seem to have a right to be worried – they are significantly more liable to be female smokers with a family history of cardiovascular disease, says a study in the *British Journal of General Practice* (2003, 53; 495: 790).

BLOOD-PRESSURE BLUNDERS

There is one further reason why medics can send your blood pressure soaring. They often don't take the readings correctly. Nearly three-quarters of health-care workers fail to put your arm in the right position when taking blood-pressure readings, and this can make the result up to 10 per cent higher, says a report in the *Annals of Internal Medicine* (8 January 2004).

Investigators from the University of California, San Diego School of Medicine and the Medical College of Wisconsin say 73 per cent of health-care workers fail to use the proper arm position and blood-pressure cuff positions.

Just so you know, the researchers argue that the correct procedure is to position the patient's elbow at a right angle to the body with elbow flexed at heart level. In any other position, the reading can be so inaccurately high as to prompt doctors to start giving unnecessary treatment.

DOCTORSPEAK: THE TERRIBLE TRUTH

If you ever have the misfortune to have a pair of hospital doctors talking across your bedridden body, listen carefully. That jumble of jargon and acronyms could reveal that they don't like you, or that your outlook is less than hopeful. Sincere condolences if you ever hear yourself described as CTP – that's 'circling the plughole'.

Doctors from hospitals in London and Cambridge compiled a list of slang terms used in British medicine in *Ethics & Behavior* (2003, 13; 2: 173). Here they are, along with a few other old medical favourites:

Betty *Someone with diabetes*
Cheerioma *Patient with a highly aggressive, malignant cancer*
CLL *Chronic low life*
Coffin dodger *Elderly patient*
Departure lounge *Geriatric ward*
Digging for worms *Varicose vein surgery*
FLK *Funny-looking kid (in babies' notes)*
Freud squad *Psychiatrists*
Gassers *Anaesthetists*
GPO *Good for parts only*
Guessing tube *Stethoscope*
House red *Blood*
LOBNH *Lights on but nobody home*
Oligoneuronal *Of low intellect*
Pest control *Term applied to psychiatrists by casualty officers*
PFO *Pissed, fell over*
PRATFO *Patient reassured and told to fuck off*
Removal men *Department of care of elderly people*
Rose cottage *Mortuary*
Rule of five *If more than five orifices are obscured by plastic tubing, the patient's condition is considered critical*
Slashers *General surgeons*

Treat'n'street *Emergency department's term for quick patient turnaround*

TUBE *Totally unnecessary breast examination*

DAMMIT, YOU DIED OF THE WRONG DISEASE

Diagnoses are a wonderful thing – the doctor has, with the benefit of science, technology, centuries of knowledge and the investigative skill of an Agatha Christie detective, divined that you are *bona fide* ill. It is a shame then that their chances of getting the diagnosis right seem no better than about 50–50.

That is the conclusion of researchers in Birmingham, UK, who examined the post-mortem notes of patients who had died in an intensive-care unit to discover what had actually killed them, and then compared this with the doctors' original diagnoses.

They report in *Critical Care* (1 March 2002) that their study of 38 patients over a three-and-a-half year period found that in 47 per cent of the cases doctors had missed the main cause of death. Only 42 per cent of the patients' notes showed a complete agreement between the diagnosis and the post-mortem findings.

The doctors had most frequently failed to diagnose cancer, heart-valve failure, infections and pulmonary embolism. Not exactly obscure stuff. And this was in people lying in beds for the critically ill. 'Misdiagnosis may have led to unnecessary early death (if known for reversible causes) or unnecessary prolongation of life where terminal disease was present,' the researchers conclude. Normally, of course, doctors get to bury their mistakes.

HARD-HEARTED MEN

Any self-respecting hypochondriac is nigh certain to avoid donating blood, what with all those germs, and the lurking fear that you may somehow bleed to death. But keeping your plasma to yourself could increase your chance of arterial disease.

Kansas University Medical Center researchers claim that, unlike women, men don't get the chance to get potentially harmful iron out of their blood through menstruating. So males store it up – possibly harming their arteries. But, they report in the journal *Heart* (1997, 78; 2: 188), donating blood twice a year can help solve the problem.

PET THERAPY

They don't just bite the
hand that feeds

EIGHT DOGS, ONE HORSE, ONE DONKEY ...

Animals responsible for severely biting the penises of two men and eight boys rushed to Sao Paulo University Hospital between 1983 and 1999, as reported in the *Journal of Urology* (2000, 165; 1: 80).

LOVE LIZARD

Cuddly iguana? Some people swear the cold-blooded tongue-flickers are loving companions. But it can go too far when iggy wants to get jiggy.

The Journal of the American Association of Reptile Veterinarians (Vol. 1, 1991) exposed 18 cases of sexual assault by iguana in American homes.

The pattern behind the attacks was so similar that it was highly unlikely to have been coincidence. In each case, the bond between animal and owner was unusually intimate. Some owners slept, showered and ate with their pets.

In each case the animal was the sole iguana in the home, all attacks took place in the breeding season and the offending reptile was male and sexually mature. The victims were women heads of the household, within childbearing age and either menstruating or just about to start at the time of the attack.

The authors speculate that one or more components of human sexual pheromones are identical or similar to those occurring in iguanas. A cage, they suggest, is the answer.

BEWAREWOLF

Lycanthropy makes people believe they have been transformed into animals. It is sufficiently widespread to have spawned a self-help group in the US called Werewolves Anonymous.

YAPPY OR SNAPPY?

Dogs kill 20 Americans each year and injure 585,000. The types of dogs most likely to bite, according to the Centers for Disease Control and Prevention, are:

German shepherds
Chow chows
Collies
Male or unneutered dogs
Dogs belonging to a household with children
Dogs chained up in a yard.

The safest are:

Golden retriever
Standard poodle

(From *Pediatrics*, June 1994)

NICE DOGGIE ... ER

The fatal dog-bite attack league table for the quarter-century from 1979 to 1998, compiled for the *Journal of the American Veterinary Medical Association* (2000, 217; 6: 836), shows that of the top human-killing breeds, more than half were pit-bull types or rottweilers.

But think also *location, leash, location*: 58 per cent involved unrestrained dogs on their owners' property; 24 per cent involved unrestrained dogs off their owners' property; and 17 per cent involved restrained dogs on their owners' property.

FELINE FEAR FACTOR

You are much safer with a cat. But somehow it may be much more traumatic to be viciously mauled by a mewling assailant called Fluffy or Tinkerbell. UK Department of Health figures show that 18,000 people were injured in cat-related incidents in the year 2002 alone.

And when Kitty gets vicious, things quickly go all Stephen King. Pensioner Leila Johnstone, 66, was asleep when her puss, Susie, launched a frenzied attack. It sank its claws into Johnstone's forehead and ripped her arm through to the bone. Johnstone thinks her pet may have been spooked by a ginger tom sitting outside her flat.

'I woke up with this black thing hanging on to me. I fought her but she still clung on. I didn't know what was happening and I was terrified. There was blood everywhere and I thought I was done for,' she tells the Scottish *Daily Record* (29 August 1997).

Johnstone, of Castlemilk, Glasgow, managed to break free but Susie chased her and gouged her leg before Johnstone shut her in a room. Johnstone was then rushed to the Glasgow Victoria Infirmary.

'I still don't feel right,' she tells the *Record*. 'I'm feeling sick and dizzy all the time. And I can't believe the cat did this. I'm just glad it didn't happen to any of my grandchildren.'

Susie the cat was put down.

The tragic fight between grandmother and cutely named pet puss is, it seems, a common factor in such incidents.

Edna Brown, 83, was mauled so badly by her tabby cat called McGuinty that she needed 27 stitches. Police who attended the incident at Elmira told the *Toronto Star* (11 August 2000) they had seen less blood at murder scenes.

'He just grabbed my legs,' Brown says of her grey-and-white assailant. 'I pulled him off and I threw him into the corner and then he attacked again. He wouldn't let go.'

Brown managed to shove the hissing pet into her apartment and ran out. She then collapsed, the blood from wounds to both ankles and her right arm pouring down the hallway steps. 'I don't know why he attacked me. We were best of friends,' she says.

Dr Gerard Hess of the local Kitchener-Waterloo Humane Society tells the paper it is not uncommon for cats to turn on their owners. He gets such reports about once a month.

Just about anything, it seems, can spark off cat rage. When Cocoa Puff, a four-year-old Siamese, attacked a family and sent them fleeing from their home, jealousy was blamed as the motive.

The frenzy left Laurel Mancini, her husband and children bleeding from deep scratches and bites. The family told the *Calgary Sun* (15 May 2002) they believe the cat became agitated after the Mancini family's babysitter admired their new kitten. 'The cat just snapped,' says Robert Mancini.

So make sure you never do this: Gerard Daigle, 80, lost half a litre of blood and required stitches after his cat, Touti, launched a frenzied attack, reports

Australia's *Gold Coast Bulletin* (14 July 2001). The provocation? Daigle was giving his pet parrot a shower when he inadvertently sprayed Touti the cat with water.

WHO GETS BIT

Men are at greater risk of being bitten by dogs, adult women by cats and young girls by horses, says a two-year casualty-department study in Oslo, reveals *Tidsskr Nor Laegeforen* (1998, 118; 17: 2614).

WATCH WHAT YOU PAT

- *Pet cats and dogs can harbour salmonella, camphylobacter and other stomach-poisoning bacteria. Their paws can carry high levels of multi-resistant staphylococcus aureus (MRSA).*
- *Rabbits can spread listeriosis, salmonella and even bubonic plague*
- *Horses can carry Lyme disease, salmonella and encephalitis*
- *Around 38 per cent of tortoises in Britain are infected with salmonella*
- *Town pigeons can spread at least ten serious infectious diseases, from mild food poisoning to viral encephalitis.*

(Sources: Dr Robert Baker, research fellow in infectious diseases at the Centre for Infectious Diseases, in central London (*Independent*, 14 October 1999); International Scientific Forum on Home Hygiene (2002))

BIG H HISTORY

From Greek ribs to a possible cure

It is easy to believe hypochondria is so deeply wired into the human brain that it has always been with us – and always will be. According to the writer, Aldous Huxley: 'Directly or indirectly, most of our physical ailments and disabilities are due to worry and craving. We worry and crave ourselves into high blood pressure, heart disease, tuberculosis, peptic ulcer, low resistance to infection, neurasthenia, sexual aberrations, insanity, suicide. Not to mention the rest.'

Perhaps that's a bit strong, but it is reckoned that hypochondriac patients form between 4 per cent and 6 per cent of the average community doctor's workload, says Dr Brian Fallon, an associate professor of psychiatry at Columbia University in New York and co-author of *Phantom Illness: Shattering the Myths of Hypochondria*. Other studies put the figure even higher.

But where did hypochondria come from? I like to imagine that the condition stretches back to our early hunter-gatherer ancestors, recently down from the trees and finding life on the ground so fraught that it has got them complaining of flint-napper's elbow and post-Jurassic stress disorder. The H-word itself comes somewhat later – courtesy of the Ancient Greeks. It derives from *hypochondrium* and refers to a specific place in the body, notably *hypo* (under) and *chondros* (the cartilage of the ribs). This anatomical description seems first to have been used by Hippocrates in 4 BC.

GREEK HEALTH FREAK

Galen of Pergamon used it to describe stomachy disorders and, because the Greeks believed abdominal organs were the source of disordered emotions, hypochondrium started to take on its second, more popular meaning – disease obsession – during the second century AD. Over the next 400 years were added its best-loved attributes: preoccupation with disease, inexplicable periods of anxiety and nightmares. The early doctors also linked it to melancholia, which may be a wise deduction – modern medical wisdom says many hypochondriacal patients may also be clinically depressed.

In seventeenth-century Europe, hypochondria started to be used to describe a depressive disorder that was characterized by indigestion and vague whingy pains. Leeches, those aspirins of the Middle Ages, were the preferred treatment. One can imagine the good apothecary scribbling busily on a parchment in order to avoid meeting the eyes of his persistently incurable patient and saying, 'Just take two leeches a day, and if it doesn't clear up in a fortnight come back and see me again.'

HIP TO BE HYP

A good dose of leeching should have been enough to deter any hypochondriac from complaining too loudly, but instead the condition actually became fashionable across pestilence-ridden Renaissance Europe. For this, says Susan Baur, the author of

Hypochondria: Woeful Imaginings, you can blame the Italian arty in-crowd. They threw out the age-old convention that rudely wholesome gladiatorial types were the guys to have at your party. Instead they invented the idea that pale neurotics were interesting and cool, thus anticipating the New York punk scene by 300 years and setting up the classic jock vs nerd confrontation central to any frat-house movie.

THE ENGLISH MALADY

The fashion for writhingly neurotic tubercular screw-ups rapidly spread northwards to its fog-bound natural incubator – Britain. In 1733, George Cheyne, a pop doctor of the period, wrote the early hypochondriac's handbook, *The English Malady: a treatise of nervous diseases of all kinds, as spleen, vapours, lowness of spirits, hypochondriacal and hysterical distempers, etc.* Cheyne blamed the condition on 'The moisture of our air, the variableness of our weather, the richness and heaviness of our food, the wealth and abundance of the inhabitants, the inactivity and sedentary occupations of the better sort (among whom this evil mostly rages) and the humour of living in great, populous and consequently unhealthy towns.'

Cheyne declared that roughly one third of his countrymen suffered from hypochondria and hysteria. He added that the disease tended to afflict persons of greater intelligence and upper social class, and the condition became so chic that it came to be called 'hyp'. An anxious, gloomy temperament became both a sign of high intelligence and a must-have fashion accessory. The writers Boswell and Johnson were among the hippest of the hyppies.

VICTORIAN VICE

It was not until the following century, though, that hypochondria came to be narrowly defined as an excessive fear of illness. Historians speculate that the morbid Victorian obsession with sickness grew in harness with the development of medical science, which helpfully kept discovering more and more new illnesses and health threats for us all to worry about – while technology, sanitation and medical advances actually made huge leaps in making our lives far safer than ever before.

HYPOCHONDRIA CURED?

Psychologists have announced some potentially devastating news for hypochondriacs, or at least for the medics, therapists, life gurus and pharmaceutical companies that profit from them: there may be a cure for hypochondria (or what in modern polite-speak is increasingly being defined as 'health anxiety').

Arthur J. Barsky, previously cited in this book for his work on the nocebo effect, reports in March 2004 that cognitive behavioural therapy can significantly alleviate hypochondriacal fears. He and colleagues at the Brigham and Women's Hospital and Harvard Medical School, Boston, gave six weeks' worth of 90-minute psychotherapy sessions to patients whose reported medical symptoms could not be explained by any real illness.

Barsky reports in the *Journal of the American Medical Association* (2004, 291; 12: 1464) that he studied 187 hypochondriacal patients for a year: 102 were given psychotherapy, while the rest were run through the medical system. Unfortunately, a quarter of the psychotherapy patients left the programme as soon as they learnt it was offering a mental rather than physical cure for the problems they perceived. 'Most hypochondriac people never will go to a psychiatrist,' says Barsky. 'They will say, "I don't need to talk about this, I need somebody to stick a biopsy needle in my liver, I need that CAT scan repeated."'

Nevertheless, those who stuck with the six psychotherapy sessions explored the five factors that can lead people to blow their bodily symptoms out of all proportion and then to convince themselves they have a serious disease. The factors are: their hypervigilance about bodily functions; their beliefs about what causes their apparent symptoms; their mood; the circumstances that start them obsessing; and their need to behave like sick people. The sessions also encouraged patients to stop habits that worsen their symptoms, such as Googling for disease information on the internet, browsing newspaper obituaries and reading books like this one.

A year after the weekly 90-minute sessions, Barsky reports that almost 57 per cent of the patients had 'significantly lower levels of hypochondriacal symptoms, beliefs, and attitudes and health-related anxiety'. That represents a reasonably encouraging increase over the 32 per cent of hypochondriacal patients whose lives improved after going through the normal medical system – though in both sets of patients, their actual physical symptoms did not go away. But then we all get back tweaks, stomach growls, headaches and so on.

It seems that this intensive approach could therefore work for a sizeable number of people whose hypochondria is so severe it can wreck their lives – and it certainly seems to work much better than the traditional medical response: either ignore them or give them a tablet – or even an operation – to make them go away.

Individuals might be curable. But what about a wholesale remedy for today's hypochondriacal society? Would Western civilization be able to carry on without empty threats to obsess about? We might simply dance free of our old fearful shackles and live long lives of stressless joy. Given *Homo sapiens'* innate drive to fixate on threat and danger, it seems far more likely that we would end up like the urban myth about hedgehogs, which says that if you rid them of their fleas, they start to suffer withdrawal symptoms.

A constant barrage of newly reported threats to our well-being does rather jazz up our sometimes mundane lives and distract us from difficult spiritual questions such as that old nagger, 'What is the meaning of it all?' Orwell's 1984 featured global war as a constant distractor and motivator. We have our health to worry about. Shame it makes us ill.

WORLD OF WORK

Hi ho, hi ho, it's off to croak we go

DEATH BY CORRUPT COLLEAGUES

Better hope your workmates and organization are all free of scandal. If they aren't, your chances of killing yourself could leap.

It's called **Di Pietro syndrome** and was identified after mass-media coverage of a local-government bribes case in Italy at the end of the 1980s caused widespread suspicion of people who worked in public services. This, say researchers at Policinico Hospital, Milan, exacerbated pre-existing psychiatric problems in administrators and workers, as shown by the suicide of five local council managers after they were interviewed by investigators.

One, a 35-year-old health administrator in a Milanese hospital, jumped in front of a train. He survived, and told how he had developed delusions, anxiety and depression and guilt about imagined – and wholly non-existent – shortcomings in his work performance, after he had read about the arrest of managers in the city's health-care system. The irrational fear of being discovered and jailed prompted the suicide bid, reports the *Psychiatric Bulletin* (1993, 17; 4: 246).

EARLY GRAVE PLEASE, DRIVER

Driving a bus or taxi boosts your risk of heart attack, claim Swedish researchers.

Professional drivers are also more likely to smoke and be overweight, but the increased risk could not be explained by these or other known risk factors, says Dr Carolina Bigert of Karolinska Hospital in Sweden.

Bus drivers are more than twice as likely to have a heart attack as men who had never worked as professional drivers. Taxi drivers' risk is only slightly lower, says the report in *Epidemiology* (2003, 14; 3: 333).

Dr Bigert says this may be due to stress, but she isn't sure. That's helpful.

HAIRDRESSER'S NIPPLE

Beware if you are a woman hairdresser. It may not be just the customers' generosity that leads you to getting bigger tips. Doctors at Birmingham's Queen Elizabeth Hospital who treated a woman patient for painful breast infections claimed their place in the annals of medical history by reporting the first known case of hairdresser's nipple in the *British Medical Journal* (1988, 297; 6664: 1641).

They discovered the phenomenon when they found that sharp little male hairs had penetrated her areolas, causing them to become infected and inflamed. This, they concluded, had been caused by her brushing too closely to her clients, whose coarse stubble had penetrated her clothes.

THIS JOB KILLS ME

The top professions for suicide risk are:

Dentists (poisoning)
Vets (poisoning)
Farmers (guns)

Hanging is statistically popular with librarians. Perhaps because it's quiet and tidy.

If you are male, single or widowed and aged between 15 and 44, then you are in the highest risk group for killing yourself, says the UK government report, *Trends in Suicide in England and Wales, 1982–96* (Office of National Statistics).

If you do plan on ending it all, be warned that the old hosepipe-from-the-exhaust method is out of fashion – and less effective than ever. The report says the fall in suicides from poisoning by motor-vehicle exhaust gas since the early 1990s is due to the growing number of cars fitted with catalytic converters.

MUSE MISERY

Tortured artists have a grim old time of it. But writers and painters have much higher rates of suicide than musicians. Perhaps the tunes keep your spirits high, suggest Italian researchers in the *Psychological Report* (2001, 89; 3: 719).

SEASONAL SUICIDE

Getting out in the fresh air might cheer you up, but then again, working in the great outdoors seems to have a strange seasonal effect on suicide rates. Finnish psychiatrists have discovered that farmers and forestry workers kill themselves most in the cheerful countryside season of spring and commit the fewest suicides in dismal, cold winter.

Perhaps more predictably, people who work indoors kill themselves most frequently in summer, they report in the *Journal of Affective Disorders* (2002, 70; 2: 197). Those open office windows sometimes just look too tempting.

BUSINESS TRAVEL TRAUMA

Jetsetting is not all glamour – in fact those tempting overseas trips may prove rather sickening for travellers and their stay-at-home spouses.

Researchers at the World Bank, Washington, D.C., studied more than 10,000 of their staff to see if global travel harmed their health. The results show that their rates of health-insurance claims are significantly higher than non-travelling staff.

The biggest problem is psychological disorders, followed by infections – and the more the employees travel, the more problems they have. Interestingly though, while male business travellers report an 80 per cent increase in illnesses, the women's ill-health rate is up by only 18 per cent, says the research in *Occupational and Environmental Medicine* (1997, 54; 7: 499).

But it is not only the travellers who suffer. If you are the spouse of a global business-trotter, your chances of falling ill also increase considerably, the researchers reveal in the same publication (2002, 59; 3: 175). Business trippers' husbands and wives are 16 per cent more likely to need medical treatment for physical and mental illness, their study finds.

The spouses suffer three times the rate of stress-related psychological disorders seen in non-travellers' partners. And they also have a much higher rate of skin and stomach diseases – which may indicate that the travellers bring home some unfortunate souvenirs. What the World Bank occupational-health researchers could not explain, however, is why travellers' spouses also develop a significantly higher number of cancers.

DOWNSHIFT DISASTER

Tempted by the dream of dropping out of the promotion race to pursue a more balanced life? Perhaps you should think again. Folk wisdom might believe that high-status, stressy business leaders are heading for an early demise. But it's the underdog that gets it, says Professor Robert Evans of British Columbia University.

A study of Whitehall civil servants has found that people at the bottom of the hierarchy consistently died younger than those at the top, and not because they were poorer or had less apparently healthy lifestyles. Over ten years, those in the lowest grades had three times as great a likelihood of dying as those at the top.

Similar patterns were found among wild baboons in the Serengeti in East Africa. Social strain is apparently to blame. 'What really bothers subordinates is not being attacked by a leopard, or even worrying about being attacked by a leopard,' Evans told the British Association's science festival in September 1994. 'It is being yawned at by a higher-ranking male at a distance of 3ft.'

From the Serengeti to Whitehall, the professor perceives a similar effect, where being an underling causes hormonal stress that could help explain the increased incidence of disease. 'What seems to be harmful is the chronic strain that comes from being subjected to frequent and unpredictable attack, both physical and particularly psychological,' he says.

SUPERVISOR STROKE

If the slacking doesn't get you, your boss might. Working under someone you consider to be an unfair manager could increase your risk of heart attack or stroke, claims a study of healthcare workers. Your blood pressure really does go up if you work for someone considered routinely unreasonable, claims this experiment involving female health-care assistants.

The assistants with duff supervisors had 15mm Hg higher systolic and 7mm Hg higher diastolic blood pressure than colleagues who felt more fairly managed. How bad is that? An increase of 10mm Hg in systolic and 5mm Hg in diastolic blood pressure is associated with a 16 per cent increased risk of coronary heart disease and a 38 per cent increased risk of stroke, says the report, in the *Journal of Occupational and Environmental Medicine* (2003, 60; 7: 468).

The research authors, at Buckinghamshire Chilterns University College's department of human sciences, say creating happier workplaces could prove a cheap way of cutting cardiovascular disorders. But then the employees end up living long enough to start draining the company pension fund.

MAIMED BY BOREDOM

It's a pretty humdrum existence, being the highest form of sentient creature on possibly the only planet in the universe capable of supporting life. No wonder so many of us suffer from occupational tedium, a newly identified sickness hazard. Studies at the University of Northumbria have found that bored people have more days off sick than any other group.

Maybe they are just slackers who would rather feed the ducks than sit shifting paper around their desks. Or perhaps they are suffering from **underload syndrome**. Dr Martyn Dyer-Smith, a psychologist at the University of Northumbria, warns, 'Boredom has exactly the same effect on the body as stress. People who are normally busy can become ill when they don't have enough to do, because it sends their levels of stress hormones shooting up.'

The *Sunday Times* (2 February 2003) listed the most common health complaints triggered by underload syndrome – headaches, fatigue and recurrent infections, as well as mild depression. It added, 'Research shows that highly strung people and those who are always on the go are most at risk. High-flyers are particularly vulnerable because they have perfected their skills and therefore are able to perform their jobs with little effort.'

CLING-ON CRISIS

Maybe you should hang on to your job throughout the economic storms and tempests known as recession and redundancy. At least it will be exciting. But then again, surviving a downturn with your career intact may only serve to accelerate your appointment with the Grim Reaper.

Seven-and-a-half years after a big round of recessionary cutbacks in Finnish councils, statisticians examined the fates of 22,430 Finnish council employees who had managed to keep their full-time jobs. The figures showed their death rates from heart attacks and strokes had doubled, particularly in the first four years after the redundancies – the period when people are most likely to die after an event that causes shock or grief.

The study, led by the Finnish Institute of Occupational Health in four towns in Finland – Espoo, Turku, Vantaa, and Raisio – suggests the increased death rates are due to the fact that the staff who hung on to their jobs had to work harder to ensure their organizations provided the same level of service.

At the same time they were left feeling very insecure about their employment prospects. The remaining workers also felt they did not have much control over their careers. If you subject rats in a lab to those types of stresses, they soon fall over.

If it is any consolation, the *British Medical Journal* report (2004, 328; 7439: 555) points out that the risk of cardiovascular death among the people who had been made redundant was even higher than that among those who kept their jobs. Either way, human beings don't seem well built to survive recessions.

BOOM OF DOOM

You might expect that economic good news would boost your health, wealth and happiness. But Swedish research shows it can land you in hospital. Sickness and hospital claims jump if the company you work for starts to expand.

The study, in the *Lancet* (2004, 363; 9416: 1193), says that when companies increase their workforce by 18 per cent or more, the long-term sickness absence among existing staff rises significantly.

Their examination of more than 24,000 individual cases from Swedish work surveys from 1989 to 1999 found that women working in the public sector are most at risk of **upsizing trauma**. The surprised researchers speculate that office 'growing pains' such as organizational instability, difficulty finding decent new employees and longer queues in the canteen may increase existing workers' stress.

Marxists might like to conclude from all the above studies that, whichever way you work it, capitalism kills.

OFFICE SMOG

You might have paused to worry about the ozone that old fax machines chuff out, but have you ever thought about the dust storms of dead skin, crumbling cosmetics, scalp creatures, hair yeasts and foot funguses that our colleagues create?

David Bodanis, an Oxford University social theory lecturer, warns that vacuuming office carpets flings up colonies of microscopic dust mites living there. The mites' anal pellets shatter as they get pulled into the vacuum cleaner, to be propelled as fragments into the air. The pellets contain digestive enzymes from the mites' guts, which can irritate many workers' eyes and lungs.

Your fellow workers are constantly sloughing off bits of their bodies, says Bodanis, the author of *The Secret Garden* and *The Secret House*. Cosmetics crumble and talc slabs tear off and float loose. Nail polish evaporates and clothing fibres scrape away. We bring other things into the office from home: soil fragments, bits of pet fur, broken-off leaf hairs and large numbers of tiny, amputated insect limbs.

We shed many thousands of skin flakes a minute. Sweat particles and leftover soap fragments work through small gaps in our clothes. Then there are scalp creatures, hair yeasts and often even foot and other fungi. There is also all the stagnant carbon dioxide we breathe out, as well as the streams of methane and hydrogen sulphide bubbles we vent. Heat from our blood vessels provides constant gusts of warm air that rise from our bodies, lifting chunks of clothing, skin and cosmetics up to ceiling height.

We eject, on average, about 2.5 saliva droplets per word, so a few hours of cross-desk chatting at a steady 30 words per minute sling out 15,000 droplets per person. These may spend an hour or more bobbing around before sinking. A number will have more dangerous types of staphylococci, and if there's been a sneeze anywhere within metres of you, it will eject a million or more droplets. Viruses in them can float around, remaining alive, for 30 minutes or more.

Ever thought about working from home?

PRICE OF FLAME

Running away to the circus may seem the answer. All that glamour, the sawdust, the tigers and the trapeze acts – and one or two personal perils you may not have considered.

Fire-eating for example. Once you've got the hang of it, and your eyebrows and nostril hairs have grown back, it should be straightforward. Swiss medics, however, warn that performers run a high risk of hydrocarbon pneumonitis – or as the doctors from the Medizinische Klinik, Bezirksspital Dornach, prefer to call it, **fire eater's lung**.

This is caused by inhaling petrol fumes too often and can lead to coughs, breathing trouble, chest pains and fever, they report in the *Schweiz Medizinische Wochenschrift* (1994, 5; 124(9): 362). The patient they studied also developed a nasty chest infection and was seriously ill for three weeks. He recovered after two months, but presumably didn't fancy lighting up again after that.

PLANET PANIC

It's a nasty old world out there

MOON MANIA

Werewolves are the least of your worries. The full moon increases your chance of being assaulted, poisoned, committing suicide, being hospitalized for psychiatric disorders – or getting bitten by dogs.

Doctors studied crime patterns over a 5,478-day period from January 1978 to December 1982 in three Indian towns – one rural, one urban and one industrial. They found that the mean crime rate was at its lowest seven days after a full moon, when 0.4 crimes were reported per day. On the full-moon day it shot up to an average of 1.4 crimes.

The study authors, from Patna Medical College in India, are particularly interested in cases of poisoning, and suggest that, 'The increased incidence of crimes on full-moon days may be due to "human tidal waves" caused by the gravitational pull of the moon.' How so? They say that the human body is around 50 per cent to 60 per cent water, and that the full moon's gravitational pull creates a physical tide in people. At high tide, the researchers argue, people tend to get out of hand and start dropping poison into the curries of folk they don't like.

Their article, in the *British Medical Journal* (1984, 289; 6460: 1789), cites previous research in the *Psychological Report* showing that suicides and psychiatric admissions rise at full moons, and a study in the *Journal of Clinical Psychiatry* which reports that aggressive incidents also multiply. Full moons do, however, seem to prompt a reduction in the number of women attempting to poison themselves, say toxicologists in the *Medical Journal of Australia* (1993, 159; 11–12: 786). It is the new moon that causes problems – self-poisoning cases go up by a quarter, they report.

This might all sound like lunacy, but the research is further supported by Dr Peter Perkins, a Bournemouth general practitioner, in the *Journal of Epidemiology and Community Health* (1994, 48; 3: 323). He says his interviews with 79 general practitioners show their emergency calls increase by 3 per cent when there is a full moon, and drop to 6 per cent below average when there is a new moon. A decade previously, similar research showed a link between full moons and urinary retention in men with prostate trouble.

Then there is a report in *Family Practitioner* (2000, 17; 6: 472), where doctors at the Nuffield Institute for Health's Centre for Research in Primary Care studied the 'so-called **Transylvania hypothesis**', and found a 3.6 per cent increase in people coming to GP surgeries at full moons – which they describe as 'small but statistically significant'.

Doctors at the Institute of Preventive and Clinical Medicine in Bratislava, Slovakia, say their study of gout attacks between 1972 and 1994 shows that they peak under new and full moons. They report in *Medical Hypotheses* (2000, 55; 1: 24) that they have also seen similar patterns with bronchial asthma in children.

It looks like the Apollo astronauts had a lucky escape.

BARKING MAD

But it is not just humans who go strange under full moons, say accident and emergency unit doctors in Northern England, who studied the pattern of patients coming into casualty at Bradford Royal Infirmary between 1997 and 1999. In all, 1,621 new patients had been bitten by animals – 1,541 dog bites, 56 cat bites, 13 horse bites and 11 rat bites.

The lowest day for bites was the seventh after a full moon, where 41 bite victims were admitted over ten lunar cycles. The highest was the full moon, when 119 victims came into casualty. 'The rise in incidence seemed to accelerate a few days before a full moon, peaking sharply on the day of a full moon before falling away rapidly,' says the report in the *British Medical Journal* in December (2000, 321; 7276: 1559).

ILL WINDS

The *Lancet* in 2000 reports that the weather, as well as the moon, may have an important influence on health emergencies. In 1999, it says, the number of hospital admissions due to acute asthma attacks tended to rise after there had been a thunderstorm. It speculates that this may be due to a combination of high temperature, high humidity, high pollen counts and poor air quality. Or perhaps once again it is the fault of all that water sploshing around in our bodies.

FATAL MAGNETIC ATTRACTION

On the other hand, it may be that Earth's magnetic field is threatening your life.

Despite the wealth of knowledge built up by the world's cardiologists, nearly a third of heart-related deaths still cannot be explained by known risk factors, argue Israeli doctors. So they looked skywards and earthwards to examine if cardiac deaths are related to sunspots, changes in solar radiation or changes in Earth's magnetic activity.

They used statistics of death rates among Lithuanians (of all people) over a ten-year period and claim they found that the total monthly number of heart fatalities was 'significantly linked' with levels of activity in Earth's geomagnetic field. This, they add, was particularly true among people aged between 65 and 74.

We should be cheered by one piece of good news, though: the team from Rabin Medical Centre reports in *Biomedical Pharmacotherapy* (2002, 56; 2: 301s) that accident levels go down when sunspots are more active.

MOTOR MISERY

Perhaps it is not planet Earth's magnetic effect that causes heart deaths. Italian researchers suggest it could be the fault of electric fields caused by something much more mundane.

The Rome University physicians say that mortality figures from hospitals in St Petersburg, Russia, show that heart-attack death rates fall by one-and-a-quarter times at weekends. They looked for correlations with electric storms on Earth and in space, and found no link.

Instead they suggest, in *Biofizika* (1998, 43; 4: 623), that our exposure to trains' and trams' electric motors when commuting to work may expose us to low-frequency magnetic fields that are powerful enough to bring our tickers to an unscheduled halt.

STAR STRICKEN

Too down to earth? Let's go up into the heavens: perhaps the puppet-strings of our fickle fates are being tugged by distant galaxies. Our star-signs can determine our deaths, warn astrologists.

According to medico-astrological research, the tall, dark stranger that Virgoans will meet today could be the county coroner, or so suggests a Liverpool University study of local death records in *Medical Science Law* (2003, 43; 2: 111). It claims that people born under Virgo have the highest risk of committing suicide by hanging themselves.

People born under summer-month star signs have the highest chance of suffering any kind of violent death, says the report. But Sagittarians and Scorpions can take heart – they are the Zodiac signs with the least danger of doing themselves in.

On the other hand, Auburn University sociologists say in *Perception and Motor Skills* (1988, 66; 2: 461) that only those born under the most negativistic sign of Pisces have a significantly raised risk of feeling suicidal.

HORROR SCOPE FOR MEN

In another study, the Manchester University Management School marketing lecturer Vincent-Wayne Mitchell says that UK government statistics on population behaviour show that men's health risks are related to their birth signs.

Mitchell says that men born under Aries, Aquarius and Pisces are more likely to smoke, and he claims this is because they are less open to persuasion about health risks. Men with more outgoing star signs, such as Gemini, are more likely to have an alcohol problem, because they think drinking is sociable, he says in the *Journal of Consumer Marketing* (1997, 14; 2: 113).

HAYFEVER? THAT'S NOTHING

Allergies are all the rage. But they can, it seems, get much wilder than simply making you sneeze. Take Jenny Wyatt, for example, who lives in Richmond, Surrey. She says she is **allergic to electricity**. 'It started in 1999 when my family bought a fridge-freezer and I started experiencing strange symptoms. Within minutes of walking into the kitchen I'd feel dizzy and I had mood swings – bursting into tears and feeling depressed.'

She says she had contracted ME after flu in 1995, and a couple of years later developed food and chemical sensitivities. She seemed to be stabilizing when the new symptoms appeared. She tells the *Independent on Sunday* (2 September 2001) that she wears magnetic insoles, cooks on a portable gas stove and can stand only muted lighting – she often uses candles.

Ena Bowles, 69, of Tonyrefail, Mid-Glamorgan, tells the same newspaper that she is **allergic to**

chemicals. 'I have one of the worst allergies to chemicals in this country. I constantly felt exhausted, had headaches and nausea. I'd have an asthma attack if I walked past the Body Shop. I was allergic to every type of asthma inhaler, so I had no help in an attack.' After a series of vaccine injections, she says she is now better, but says, 'Anything near my face has to be natural fibres. Newspapers are a problem as well – I have to wear a facemask to read them.'

Joan Stock, 79, says she is so **allergic to microchips** that she lives in a time-warp, unable to use most electrical equipment, or to travel by public transport or in modern cars. The *Bath Chronicle* (15 August 2001) reports how she watches a black-and-white valve television at her home near Bristol and drives an old Ford. She began suffering crippling headaches 20 minutes after an electronic typewriter was introduced at the office where she worked in 1975.

Tony Doherty was saved from a gaol sentence in 1986 after a court accepted his claim that he was **violently allergic to potatoes**. The full extent of his allergy only became clear when he ate two packets of potato crisps and attempted to strangle his father with a tie. The problem had not been identified before the court case. The 21-year-old County Antrim man was warned to stay away from potatoes, says the *Courier Mail* (22 September 1986).

Donna Robertson is **allergic to the 21st century**. The 55-year-old housewife tells the *Glasgow Evening Times* (16 November 2002) that she is a prisoner in her home. There are no carpets and she mops the floors with an odourless cleaner three times a day. She can't wear perfume, and neither can the rest of her family when they are within sniffing distance of her.

Her family leave their aftershaves and deodorants outside the front door. If she is exposed, she says she gets runny eyes, nausea or vomiting, chest infections and tiredness. Robertson says she suffers from **multiple chemical sensitivity**, an illness first reported in America. She says she knows one MCS sufferer who reacts to the concrete residue on the soles of people's shoes. Another has been known to fall into a coma.

LOUD-SHIRT SENSITIVENESS

The allergy phenomenon has been growing since the 1950s, when Amelia Nathan Hill set up Action Against Allergies in America and persuaded millions of people that their headaches, fatigue, palpitations, muscle weakness and a general inability to cope could all be blamed on allergy.

Hill died in 2001, having seen her message become mainstream. But the growth of allergy-fear has also prompted a growing number of sceptics to ask if the epidemic is not partly the latest bout of health hysteria that, in different incarnations, has hit the Western world from century to century. The sceptical science writer Caroline Richmond invented a spoof illness in the 1980s – **allergy to bright clothes**, and wrote to Hill warning her of it. Hill's organization publicized the illness and, before long, a small but growing group of people claimed they had it. When Hill was told it had been a joke, she insisted that bright clothes allergy really did exist, and thanked Richmond for having exposed it.

ALLERGIC TO EVERYTHING

The American illness, multiple chemical sensitivity (MCS) is a condition characterized by a gamut of allergic reactions, and frequently by the close proximity of a lawyer.

MCS is claimed to be a dysfunction of the nervous system caused by an overload of offending agents. Many sufferers claim it has ruined their lives. One woman sufferer is reported to hang her mail on a clothes line for two weeks to allow it to 'detoxify' before she can read it.

A paper from the Chemical Injury Information Network lists more than a hundred symptoms which may result from MCS. These include sneezing, itching, twitching, hoarseness, earache, high or low blood pressure, sore muscles, cramps, frequent urination, PMS, lower back ache, nausea, belching, constipation, hunger, thirst, headaches, apathy, forgetfulness, insomnia, depression, heat sensitivity, cold sensitivity, stiffness, swelling, pain in the neck, agitation and genital sweating.

The bottom of the page adds: 'Unfortunately this is not a complete list of symptoms.'

Hands up if you have not had any of those symptoms.

CAR-COLOUR KILLERS

Worried about road safety? You should be: around 3,000 people are killed in crashes every day worldwide. And you are particularly at peril if the car in your garage is painted brown, black or green.

But you could halve your chances of serious injury from an accident if your vehicle comes in a sensible shade of silver. Research conducted in New Zealand claims that drivers of silver cars face half the risk run by other car drivers of a serious accident involving injury.

Researcher Sue Furness, of the University of Auckland, says that brown, black and green cars have the highest crash risk. Red, often considered the colour of safety, is no better than blue, grey, yellow or white, according to the report in the *British Medical Journal* (2003, 327; 7429: 1455). The risk of a serious injury in yellow, grey, red, and blue cars is not so bad – and not significantly different from that in white cars.

Her research provoked a flurry of criticism about its methods, but it supports a study the previous year, reported in *Epidemiology* (2002, 13; 6: 721), which suggests that bright or light-coloured vehicles such as yellow and white are safer, particularly on open roads in daylight, because they are more visible. The study used data from the Spanish database of traffic crashes from 1993 to 1999.

But Furness, who studied 1,000 drivers in Auckland in 1998 and 1999, found silver to be safest of all. She says, 'Increasing the proportion of silver cars could be an effective strategy to reduce the burden of injury from car crashes.'

Why not go all the way and paint every car on the road silver? Perhaps we would have no crash deaths at all.

LEGAL DRUG DRIVERS

On the other hand, you would still have to look out for elderly drivers so confused by their prescription drugs that they are unlikely to notice the existence of other traffic, let alone the colour of your car.

Telling if an older person is too stoned on medication to drive is a difficult business. But one study of Canadian drivers aged from 67 to 84 found they were twice as likely to be in a serious car crash if they were on lithium to control their moods, reports the *British Medical Journal* (2004, 328: 558–559). Other studies have found similar crash statistics involving some of the millions of elderly people prescribed benzodiazepine tranquillizers.

CHRISTMAS CRASHERS

Beyond drugs and paint colours, even family festivities can cause serious road accidents, claims the RAC. The motoring organization's psychiatrists claim that car drivers are suffering 'a deadly new syndrome' – **festive auto disorder**, or FAD, reports the London *Evening Standard* (23 December 1997).

Symptoms, which strike during the season of good cheer, include extreme irritability and volatile disagreements among car occupants suffering a variety of 'stress points' connected with Christmas and the mass migration towards family turkey dinners.

'Ill-feeling and simmering discontent between family members in the close confines of festive homes can boil over at the slightest provocation once they get behind the wheel,' claims the psychologist Conrad King, who maintains that precisely 56 per cent of in-car arguments are caused by bad map reading or getting lost. Back-seat driving and unruly passengers are the next two most common causes of family fall-outs, he says.

'It is an important road-safety issue,' King says. 'The seasonal syndrome invariably involves arguments outside the car which eventually boil over in the confined space of the family saloon and cause distress on the road.'

He adds: 'People might also be aware of SAD [Seasonal Affective Disorder caused by lack of sunlight hitting the brain] and how that can lead to feeling down at this time of the year. But a combination of FAD and SAD could ruin anyone's Christmas.'

CADILLAC ARRESTS

You might be better off getting out of the car and walking. The air inside your vehicle can be more polluted than that outside – to the point where it damages your heart, warns America's Environmental Protection Agency in May 2004.

The agency measured the pollution levels in nine police officers' squad cars and tested their blood levels for signs of harmful proteins that can lead to heart blockages. The levels were consistently higher at the end of their nine-hour patrol shifts than they had been at the start.

Robert Devlin, an agency researcher, says that even when you shut your car windows and close the air vents, there can be more harmful pollution inside your cabin than out on the street. Dangerous particles from your exhaust are sucked back inside and stay there in higher concentrations. The particles can be so small – one eight-hundredth the width of a human hair – that they pass through air filters.

HEADACHE
OR TUMOUR?

What do you mean, it's not serious?

That ache, rash, pain or occasional mystery symptom could well land you in hospital – and things can go seriously downhill from there. Up to 13 per cent of patients in hospitals and doctors' surgeries may in fact be suffering from simple hypochondria, warns the Maudsley Hospital psychiatrist Oliver Howes in the *Lancet* (1998, 351; 9112: 1332).

Unfortunately, hypochondriacs are frequently mistaken by the busy doctors and nurses for people with real life-threatening illnesses. And this, ironically, causes a significant number of hypochondriacs to be made ill by being sent for unnecessary medical investigations and operations, and given unnecessary and potentially harmful drugs. So before you dial the ambulance, think at least twice ...

PERSISTENT HEADACHE OR BRAIN CANCER?

Risk rate less than 1 per cent
Something at the back of your mind tells you it's bound to be tumour. In fact this is extremely unlikely. Fewer than one in 100 people with regular headaches is found to develop a brain tumour. They are rare in the under-thirties and only about 3,500 people develop one each year in England and Wales.

Still not convinced? These are the clinical signs: severe persistent headache; vomiting – sometimes suddenly; dizziness; fits; major seizures or local twitching; partial hearing loss; loss of hearing or sense of smell; hallucinations; drowsiness; personality changes; and loss of co-ordination.

Otherwise, persistent headaches are more likely to be caused by inflamed sinuses, a misaligned jaw, migraine, tension, caffeine and hangovers. Or, of course, they could all be in the mind.

ABSENT-MINDEDNESS OR ALZHEIMER'S?

Risk rate 20 per cent
So the memory's not what it used to be. Could be serious, though it might well not be. Memory loss ranges in severity from simple absent-mindedness, through mild cognitive impairment, to full-blown whack-out dementias such as Alzheimer's.

Mild cognitive impairment is a mild form of memory loss that has been given a cruelly long and forgettable name. People with this condition may have to work harder to learn to remember things and experience a more rapid rate of memory decline than their peers. If you develop it, you have a higher than average chance of getting Alzheimer's.

The youngest people Alzheimer's strikes are generally in their late fifties. There's no sure way to detect if you have it, other than seeing your doctor if symptoms get worrying.

But there is the 'aha!' test. If you temporarily forget a word, then getting the feeling it is on the tip of your tongue, and finally recalling it with a sense of 'Aha! That's it,' is a healthy reaction. This doesn't tend to happen with mild cognitive impairment and Alzheimer's.

TESTICULAR CANCER LUMP OR NORMAL PLUMBING?

Risk rate 5 per cent

Cancer campaigners want men to rummage themselves monthly – or get a woman friend to check their balls for them. So after a bath or shower, while rolling the testicles between thumb and forefinger, you may find something worrying at the back of the scrotum. It's small, firm and tube-like. Now breathe normally. It's the epididymis. It transports sperm. Only if you find other small lumps, irregularities, enlargements or changes in firmness should you go to the surgery. Even then, its probably not a problem.

FLOATERS OR BLINDNESS?

Risk rate 1 per cent

The most common cause of disturbances in your field of vision are grey floaters – particles in the fluid at the back of the eye. People notice them more on bright days. They shift as you glance around. It's normal to have one or two per eye. Hypochondriacs tend to notice them – and worry about them – much more. But if you do suddenly notice a large number, visit an optometrist.

Flashing disturbances and double vision are a bit more worrying. If they are accompanied by mind-blitzing headaches, then it sounds like migraine. They could be a result of your coming off benzodiazepines, which are often prescribed for anxiety. They might be a symptom of high blood pressure, where visual disturbances can be accompanied by fatigue, breathlessness, ringing in the ears and headaches.

And just to cheer you up, it might just – but only might just – indicate that a brain tumour is increasing the pressure in your skull.

HEART ATTACK OR HEARTBURN?

Risk rate 5 per cent

Shockingly painful burning sensation behind the breastbone? Acid taste in the throat? Just had a stressy lunch? Probably heartburn. Excess stomach acid heads up from the stomach, causing burning behind the breast bone and an acid taste in the throat. And yes it can hurt a lot – gut juice is as corrosive as battery acid, and its production is boosted by stress.

The pain can be so severe people think they are having a coronary. This can be ruled out with a simple ECG test. Are you on first-name terms with the hospital ECG people? Take it as an early warning from your heart: being overweight and smoking makes heartburn worse, as well as massively increasing your chances of a coronary.

PALPITATIONS OR HEART FAILURE?

Risk rate 2 per cent

Heartbeat sometimes goes funny? Hypochondriacs are renowned for worrying about their heart rates. Practically everyone experiences some type of disturbed heartbeat now and then, but most don't go dashing to the doctors.

The palpitation is usually in the form of a mild flux or skipped beat. Your heart does not actually skip beats – the experience is called an ectopic heartbeat –

you are really noticing a pulse that is not strong enough to be felt, followed by a relatively forceful beat.

People who fixate on their heart rate also fear that it is running too quickly, too slowly or irregularly. Odd heart rates are called cardiac arrhythmias, though normally the arrhythmias are in the patient's head. A normal pulse is 60–80 beats a minute. Go on then, check it.

If you do have an irregular heartbeat, it could indicate that you will go on to develop more serious problems. Be worried if you have recurrent palpitations, chest discomfort, fainting, sweating, breathlessness, dizziness or confusion.

If you are still worried, cut out recognized triggers such as coffee and alcohol. And stop worrying: the ancient poets were right – emotions do make hearts flutter, and the majority of ectopic heartbeats are due to emotional stress.

ALL IN THE MIND

But that doesn't mean it ain't lethal

CORROSIVE CHARACTERS

From the ancient Greeks to Shakespeare and beyond, the concept of tragedy has focused on the idea that people carry the seeds of their own destruction. This is reinforced by modern research which claims to show that your personality can predict the disease that will kill you.

Strange results from a study of Scottish people have prompted epidemiologists to claim that your temperament may be linked to the illness you ultimately die from. The researchers examined the records of the 878 patients who died out of a population of almost 10,000 Glasgow students. The students' temperaments had been recorded by a doctor over a 20-year period from 1948 to 1968.

The report in the *Journal of Epidemiology and Community Health* (2003, 57; 11: 888) says that nearly one in ten of the original group had been found to have an 'unstable' temperament. Those who had been diagnosed as having manic depression, more fashionably called bipolar disorder, had a higher risk of dying of a heart attack. Those who had been diagnosed as being abnormally anxious were more likely to have died of cancer.

ANXIETY ATTACKS

Further evidence that you can fret yourself to death comes from a Norwegian study of more than 60,000 people, which again suggests that people prone to anxiety are more likely to get cancer. Worrying, isn't it? The eight-year survey by psychiatrists at the University of Bergen, reported in *New Scientist* (31 May 2003), found that people who score highly in anxiety tests are 25 per cent more likely to develop either cancers or abnormal cells.

FROM FRETFUL TO FORGETFUL

If that were not enough to keep you awake at night, scientists studying Alzheimer's disease say they have discovered data which indicates that people who are prone to getting distressed are more likely to develop dementia.

Researchers in Chicago analysed the results of a study of 797 people in religious orders who, at the average age of 75, were Alzheimer's-free. They were given neurological examinations and measured for their ability to worry about things on a 'Neuroticism Scale' (and we all know someone who scores ten out of ten on that).

In the following five years, 140 of the people studied started to dement. The medical researchers report, in *Neurology* (2003, 61; 11: 1479), that for every point higher up the Neuroticism Scale a person scored, their risk of Alzheimer's increased by 6 per cent. Being an intensive worrier can, it seems, double your risk of the disease, they conclude.

But why? Dr Robert Wilson, of the Rush-Presbyterian-St Luke's Medical Center in Chicago, claims long-term stress seems to create changes in the brain's hippocampus, which plays a role in memory function. Does that mean that giving people stress-busting anti-depressants will cut their risk of Alzheimer's? The doctors say they don't know.

DENTURE DEMENTIA

Perhaps the Alzheimer's risk has more to do with dentistry. Researchers writing in the *Psychiatric Bulletin* (1992, 16: 227) checked 159 patients with Alzheimer's and found that half of them had false teeth – a much larger proportion than is normal for people that age.

The researchers, from the London Institute of Psychiatry, also found an increased level of family history of dementia in patients with false teeth, which they say 'suggests a genetic predisposition towards both'. But the link may have more to do with jaws than genes.

The lead researcher, Alistair Burns, and his team also found, using brain scans, an association between false teeth and brain cells dying in the temporal lobe. This 'may be the result of reduced chewing, leading to a disuse atrophy of the limbic system', he reports.

SEASONAL SCHIZOPHRENIA

Chewing each mouthful of food 42 times might stave off Alzheimer's, but your risk of developing another common form of mental illness may come down to something as simple as your birthday.

Being born at the wrong time of year can increase your chance of developing schizophrenia, claims Dr J.M. Eagles, who studied more than 3,500 people diagnosed as schizophrenic born between 1900 and 1969. His article, in the *British Journal of Psychiatry* (1995, 167; 4: 469), reports that men born in the winter or spring months are significantly more likely to develop the disorder than men born in the rest of the year.

That correlation is getting stronger as the years go by, for reasons Dr Eagle cannot explain. He adds, however, that for women, the birthday/schizophrenia link is weak, and growing steadily weaker.

BIRTHDAY BLUES

Women's birthdays are not only bad news if they hate the idea of being yet another year older. Women are more likely to die in the week after their birthday than any other week in the year, says a study of more than two million people's deaths published in *Psychosomatic Medicine* (1992, 54; 5: 532).

Why? This phenomenon shows in fact that many women really do look forward to their birthdays. Female death rates dip in the weeks beforehand, which indicates that they are hanging on for all the birthday cards and the presents, say sociologists at the University of California, San Diego. The death rate then leaps in the following week. To be on the safe side, don't buy the birthday girl any really long books to read.

FESTIVE FATALITIES

Failing to enjoy many big celebrations could also mean you missing out on months of life. People who consider cultural events important can stay alive longer, according to a study of the mortality rates of people in religious groups around significant annual festivals.

The survey of Jewish people found that their death rates fell sharply below the expected level before Passover and rose by an equal amount above it shortly afterwards. The study in the *Lancet* (1988, 2; 8613: 728) reports that, in contrast, non-Jewish control groups showed no significant fluctuation in mortality around Passover. The pattern is most pronounced in the years when Passover falls on a weekend, when it is most likely to be celebrated by the largest number of people, say the University of California researchers.

The same team reported a similar effect two years later among Chinese people around the date of the Harvest Moon Festival which, like Passover and other major cultural and religious ceremonies, involves an annual family get-together with lots of food. The researchers found that deaths fall by a third in the weeks before the festival, and rise by a compensatory third in the weeks afterwards. The biggest dip in deaths is from strokes, followed by heart attacks and tumours.

ON THE OTHER HAND ...

Big public holidays can prove such a miserable disappointment that people's risk of killing themselves takes a big leap shortly afterwards, warns a report in *Suicide and Life Threatening Behaviour* (1999, 29; 3: 272).

Danish researchers call this the 'broken-promise effect' and say that their study of 32,000 of their compatriots over 25 years shows an increase in suicides is particularly noticeable just after the major public holidays of Christmas, Easter and Whitsun.

UNLUCKY DEATH DAYS

Days thought to signify bad luck really do prove unfortunate for the unusually high number of Japanese and Chinese people who suffer heart deaths on them.

Researchers at the University of California, San Diego, noted that the number four is considered an ill omen in Japanese and Chinese culture, particularly because it is close in sound to 'death' in some Southeast Asian languages. So they examined mortality rates on the fourth day of each month, and discovered that these are the peak days for Japanese and Chinese cardiac fatalities in hospitals.

They compared this phenomenon with death rates among white Americans – for whom the fourth of each month is just an ordinary day (with the exception, of course, of the fourth of July). The scientists report in the *British Medical Journal* (2001, 323; 7327: 1443) that it is statistically just like any other heart-death day for white America.

The researchers have christened the phenomenon the **Hound of the Baskervilles Effect**, after the Sherlock Holmes character scared to death by a ghostly dog.

The peak-death effect on the fourth of the month was not followed by a compensatory dip in heart deaths on subsequent days among Japanese and Chinese patients. So the effect might not simply hit people who were going to have a heart attack anyway. It may prey on those who would never have died around that time – had they not been scared to death by superstition, or if Japan and China had removed the number four from their calendars.

BLUE-LIPPED MONDAY

In many industrialized societies, miserable Monday mornings are a lethal problem, according to research from Germany and Italy which shows that heart attacks are most common as the week begins. Experts blame it on the stress of returning to work after the weekend: some people would rather drop dead than face another five days in the office.

The six-year study of more than 2,600 Germans, co-ordinated by researchers at the Free University of Berlin, showed that the average person has a 20 per cent higher chance of having a heart attack on a Monday than on any other day. The report, in *Circulation* (1994, 90; 1: 87), reveals that the Teutonic work ethic is no help: employed Germans have a 33 per cent higher death risk at the start of the week. Non-workers, by comparison, have no increase in risk.

Meanwhile, a study in the *European Heart Journal* (1994, 15; 7: 882) of 11,000 Italians by the Luigi Sacco Hospital in Milan has identified 8 a.m. on a Monday morning as the most stressful time for the heart, and both the German and Italian studies showed that Sunday is the least stressful point of the week for working men.

WEEKEND WOE

Monday is not the worst day for everyone, though. While Japanese men's heart-fatality rates increase by a quarter on Mondays, Japanese women's cardiac death rates jump by more than a third on Saturdays, say Osaka University doctors. They admit in *Heart* (2003, 89; 4: 398) that they are not certain of the women's precise risk factors but speculate that Saturdays signal the start of 'a stressful weekend burden for women'. Yep, hubby's home.

DEATH BY GRIEVING

You really can be killed by a broken heart, claim studies of bereaved people. That seems understandable enough, but then it gets weird, with the survey results showing that the very manner in which a loved one dies can determine the type of illness that threatens the people who mourn them.

A large-scale study of 15,000 bereaved men and women in Israel says it has found that women are 50 per cent more likely to die in the first six months after losing their partner. The rate of increase in men is 40 per cent.

Inexplicably, the lethal impact of bereavement is greater on more educated men, say the researchers from Jerusalem's Hebrew University School of Public Health and Community Medicine, in *Social Science Medicine* (2003, 56; 2: 405).

The hand-from-the-grave effect has a powerful influence in determining what illnesses bereaved people suffer, claim Dutch researchers in *Family Practitioner* (1988, 5; 4: 278). Their study of 313 bereaved people found that they are more likely to suffer a minor illness if their loved one died after a chronic illness. Bereaved people are more likely to suffer a serious illness if they have been confronted with the sudden death of a loved one, say scientists from the Nijmegen University Department of General Practice.

A study of 95,647 widowed Finns claims that in the first fortnight after losing a spouse, your risk doubles of dying of a heart attack. And in the month after having a partner die, your chances are doubled of dying in a violent incident such as an accident, the researchers write in the *American Journal of Public Health* (1987, 77; 3: 283).

TWIN TROUBLE

While the death of a partner increases your chances of dying in the following 12 months, having your twin die increases your chances of following suit in the second year after their death, warn scientists at King's College London.

Their study of Danish deaths shows the effect is stronger for identical twins – and can shorten the lives of men and women in a similar manner, they report in *Twin Research* (2002, 5; 3: 210).

CULTURE CRAZY

Is your nationality driving you mad? The American Psychiatric Association's 1997 *Diagnostic and Statistical Manual of Mental Disorders*, known by professionals as DSM-IV, lists strange syndromes peculiar to particular cultures. As any globetrotter worth his tattered backpack knows, all the world's nations are mad. They just happen to fall victim to different local madnesses.

The diagnostic manual points out that if you are a Malaysian, you may rush into the clinic suffering from **koro**, a mental illness where the sufferer is gripped by the belief that intense anxiety will make their penis (or the vulva and nipples) recede into their body and possibly cause death.

Inuit or Eskimo? **Pibloktoq** could be a problem. It's a sort of snow rage. 'During the attack, the individual may tear off his or her clothing, break furniture, shout obscenities, eat faeces, flee from protective shelters, or perform other irrational or dangerous acts,' says the manual.

As a Japanese person, you may develop **taijin kyofusho**, which can manifest itself as a dread of embarrassment.

Indian people can suffer from **jiryan**. The main symptoms are feelings of weakness and worry associated with the discharge of semen.

Chinese male? There is always the danger of **shen-k'uei**, a 'life-threatening' loss of semen leaking out in urine, again caused by anxiety.

You could try relaxing with some gentle exercise, but that could spark **Qi-gong psychotic reaction**, characterized by acute paranoid symptoms after overindulging in qi-gong, the system of exercises that forms the basis of t'ai chi.

If you are South American, a bout of **susto** – soul loss caused by a frightening experience – might be on the cards. Or you may be in line for an **ataque de nervios**, a brief outburst of dramatic disturbed behaviour following an emotional shock.

And if you hail from the Middle East, you could contract **zar**. Symptoms include shouting, laughing, hitting your head against a wall, singing or weeping, then sinking into apathetic withdrawal because you believe you are possessed by spirits. That would get you heavily sedated in the West, but 'such behaviour is not considered pathological locally,' says the manual.

The British doctors' newspaper, *Pulse* (3 June 2002), adds some more definitions for worldwide weirdness:

Brain fag is found in Nigerian and other African students. It is distinct from academic stress, and features burning or crawling sensations under the skin, visual disturbances, fatigue and disrupted concentration. **Studiation madness** is a term used in Trinidad for a similar syndrome.

Latah, meanwhile, mainly affects South East Asians and North Eurasians. Victims mimic people's posture and voices, and erupt into obscene yells when startled. An apparently identical syndrome in Siberia is called **myriachit**. In Lappland it is called **Lapp panic**.

We Westerners might think we can laugh smugly at all of this. But not so fast, says the *Pulse* author Dr Stefan Cembrowicz. Intentional drug overdoses are very rare in some cultures, for instance among Africans in the Caribbean, but they are extremely common in Europe. Likewise with anorexia. Perhaps these are also culturally bound syndromes, he suggests.

FISHY ODOUR FEAR

That niff? Is it you? If you are a woman, you are more likely to think you smell funny, according to researchers at St Mary's Hospital Medical School, London in the *Lancet* (1995, 345; 869: 1308). In response to a newspaper article about strange bodily odours, the scientists were contacted by 187 members of the public who thought they smelt rotten. Most felt they smelt of fish. Others feared they had a cheesy odour, and a few believed they had a strong tang of rotten food.

When the word spread, more than seven times more women than men got in touch, saying they smelt anything from fishy to 'vaguely unpleasant'. When questioned, how-ever, they said they were the only person to notice it – family, friends and colleagues thought nothing was amiss.

The researchers christened the problem **body malodour syndrome** and suggest that these people may suffer from cacosmia, a condition where people apparently perceive perfectly innocuous odours as offensive. Or maybe they are just surrounded by exceptionally polite people.

COLLECT THESE SYNDROMES

A syndrome is defined as a range of apparently unlinked symptoms in a patient that some sharp-eyed medic notices all share the same underlying cause. In ancient Greek, *syn drom* means to run together. Ambitious researchers know that if you can convincingly nail several symptoms together and blame them on a zeitgeisty cause, then bingo, you have carved your name in the annals of medical history – and given us all something new to worry about …

MEDIA MALAISE

Be on your guard against **information fatigue syndrome** (IFS), caused apparently by being bombarded with business data and mass media. Sufferers feel compelled to search constantly for more information. They experience anxiety and sleeplessness, as well as increasing doubt about their decision-making abilities.

The psychologist, Dr David Lewis, warned the world of IFS in a Reuters report, *Dying for Information*, in 1996. He says the syndrome is a direct result of the information revolution, and adds that having too much information can be as dangerous as having too little. His report interviewed business executives and concluded that 52 per cent suffered from it.

The illness rapidly developed its own instant victims and mythology. The *Daily Telegraph* on 12 October 1996 interviewed an IFS sufferer about her painful five-year recovery. On 20 April the following year, Edward Welsh reported in the *Sunday Times* that the syndrome had first been detected in British and American intelligence officers in the Second World War.

HISTORIC HISTRIONICS

There is real history afoot with **Stendhal's syndrome**, which strikes culture vultures gazing at Florence's Renaissance treasures. Italian doctors warn that trying to see too many artistic and historical artefacts in too short a time can cause dizziness, panic, paranoia and even madness.

It is called Stendhal's syndrome because the 19th-century French novelist is said to have been the first to write about the head-spinning disorientation some tourists experience when they encounter Florentine masterpieces. When Stendhal saw Giotto's ceiling frescoes at Santa Croce, he was overcome. 'Life was drained from me. I walked with the fear of falling,' he wrote in 1817.

But Stendhal was not the only daytripper to go all giddy. In the late 1970s, Dr Graziella Magherinie, the head of psychiatry at Florence's Santa Maria Nuova Hospital, noticed that many of the tourists who visited Florence were overcome with anything from temporary panic attacks to bouts of psychosis lasting several days. She named the temporary amnesia and disorientation Stendhal's syndrome.

You are thought most likely to be struck down by it if you are:

Aged 26 to 40
Sensitive and impressionable
A lone traveller visiting a gallery on a whim
Sightseeing without a professional guide.

Note, too, **Jerusalem syndrome**, which was identified in 1987 and is said to afflict tourists who feel oddly compelled to visit the Holy City and are overcome by encountering its ancient sites. In February 2004, Nathan Coley, a visual artist, was awarded £10,000 to investigate why between five and ten people a year find themselves clinically intoxicated by the Holy City.

BANGING HEADS

Even at home, your brain could go bang. In 1890, the phenomenon was described as being like a 'bolt driven through the head'. A 1920 report said it was 'as if something had snapped or given way in my brain'. **Exploding head syndrome** is probably quite common, but what causes it, says Dr Howard Seiden, in the *Toronto Star*, 29 March 1990, remains a medical mystery.

The main symptom is noise like an explosion, accompanied by fear or terror and sometimes a sudden flash of light. It always occurs during sleep, while a person is dropping off – and less commonly while wakening. Sufferers are mainly middle-aged or older and it is more common in women than men.

FAKE FAMILY FEAR

Do you ever get the feeling you are surrounded by phoneys? In 1923, a 53-year-old French woman complained that her family had been replaced by identical doubles. Later, she began to feel the same about friends and neighbours, and eventually feared that even she herself was being shadowed by a double. It was the first recorded case of **Capgras's syndrome**, which appears to result from damage to a 'sense of familiarity' pathway within the brain.

Since then about 300 others have been diagnosed with the syndrome. Capgras patients typically believe they live in a world of impersonators. The feeling is strongest among close family and friends but can extend to pets and places. Some years ago, a Midlands man was so sure his father had been replaced by a robot that he slashed his throat open, trying to find the wires.

Researchers believe Capgras's syndrome is caused by a failure of normal recognition processes following brain damage from a stroke, drug overdose, or some other cause. Sufferers can still recognize people and places, but no longer get the physiological buzz of familiarity that normally goes with such recognition.

SIGHTLESS SEERS

Perhaps you are blind, but don't know it. Sightless people with **Anton's syndrome** deny that they are blind. This seems to happen when two different areas of the brain have been damaged: the one needed for seeing and the one needed for knowing that you are seeing. It occurs quite suddenly, often after a stroke, and the victim of Anton's syndrome may walk around for quite some time bumping into things and having other mishaps until they become convinced something is wrong.

ANARCHIST'S ARM

Or maybe your body is about to rebel on you. In **anarchic hand syndrome**, first recognized in 1908, sufferers lose control of one hand – which acts of its own free will, causing frustration and embarrassment in equal measures. It is also known as the **Dr Strangelove syndrome**, after the 1963 film *Dr Strangelove*, in which Peter Sellers had to fight vigorously with his arm to stop it making Nazi salutes.

It is believed to be caused by damage to an area deep in the central brain, near the forehead, as a result of viruses, head injuries or strokes. There is no known cure. A case has been sent to the Dutch courts after a man claiming to have the syndrome was arrested for pinching the bottom of an air stewardess on a KLM flight. Another poor victim is reported to have been unable to stop his hand masturbating him in public, says a report in the *American Journal of Physical Medicine and Rehabilitation* (2000, 79; 4: 395).

FOREIGN ACCENT SYNDROME

So you wake up one day to find you can't help talking with a foreign accent. That will be the rare, and apparently neurological, disorder called foreign accent syndrome. In November 2003, Professor Jack Ryalis, a speech expert at the University of Central Florida reported how a local woman, Tiffany Noell, recovered from a stroke to find herself speaking with a British accent. She had never been to the UK, her family and friends found it hard to understand her, and locals kept asking where she came from. She became agoraphobic and refused to go out.

When Ryalis diagnosed her, she no longer felt mad and decided to make the condition more widely recognized and understood. That's if anyone can make out what she is saying. Things could have been worse for Noell. There have only been about 20 cases, and one of the earliest known involved a Norwegian woman recovering from shrapnel damage following the German invasion of Norway. She developed what sounded like a strong German accent and was ostracized by her community.

Cases of foreign accent syndrome have different causes and results, which can for example make a native English speaker sound Spanish or Dutch. The accent a patient develops is not dependent on any knowledge of a particular foreign language. It is rather the combination of certain changed features such as lengthening of syllables, altered pitch, or mispronounced sounds, which make a patient's pronunciation sound foreign.

Other cases include an English speaker from Massachusetts who walked away from a car accident speaking with a French accent, and probably a Gallic shrug of resignation, too. Oxford neuropsychologists have recently located some very small lesions in the brain which they claim to be the cause.

AND ON THE THIRD STROKE ...

You might have developed **horologagnosia**, a complete inability to tell the time. Dr Luke Kartsounis, of the National Hospital for Neurology and Neurosurgery in London, discovered the condition when treating a 57-year-old man who had just had a right-sided stroke.

Stroke victims often have difficulty making sense of visual information, but Dr Kartsounis reported the case in the *Journal of Neurology, Neuroscience, and Psychiatry* (1990, 30; 4: 647) because, while the sufferer scored well in language and memory tests, and could see the hands, the clock face and the numbers, he could no longer tell the time.

'If you asked him to set the hands on the clock face at a particular time, he had no problem. But he could not read what he was doing,' says Dr Kartsounis. 'He would say: the small hand is on eight, and the large hand is on 12. If you asked him what time it was, he might give – on repeated prompting – a silly answer, like eight minutes to 12.'

Fortunately, the victim started to recover after a few weeks, and became rather more clockwise.

CARTOON CRAZY

Mysterious lesions in the brain can plunge you into a strange cartoon-like fantasy world, if you suddenly develop **Lhermitte's peduncular hallucinosis**.

In 1922, the French neurologist Jean Lhermitte treated a 72-year-old woman who experienced bizarre visual hallucinations involving animals such as strange-looking chickens, people attired in odd costumes and children playing. Although the patient knew the hallucinations were not real, she would sometimes try to touch them. When she died, Lhermitte discovered the probable cause: a lesion in her midbrain.

The case was described by the neurologists Anthony Risser and Frank Powell at the 45th Annual Meeting of the American Academy of Neurology in New York in April 1993. They also reported cases of a woman patient who repeatedly saw the head of a dog or an image of an animal's body projected on to a wall of her home; a male sufferer who witnessed pictures of his grandmother flashed on the wall, as if projected in a home movie; and a man who used to watch a toy monster moving around, 'being vivid, colourful, and non-threatening'.

Other Lhermitte's patients' visions include lions jumping into the room through a window, silver and golden fish swimming below the bed, and Oriental people walking in a single line down a hallway with their hands grasped together in prayer.

The worst thing, it seems, about developing Lhermitte's peduncular hallucinosis is having to pronounce the name of your disorder. Almost everyone who has had the condition reportedly found it rather entertaining.

57 VARIETIES OF FEAR

You can, it seems, get phobic about pretty much anything. Some people are scared of otters. Others live in fear of amputees. And some folk are frightened by knees. Shona McLaren, a mother-of-two, 39, claims

Dalek-phobia has ruined her life. McLaren, of Tulli-body, Scotland, even asked members of her local church to pray for her. 'I'm a mature woman with two kids but I have always dreaded the thought of them coming anywhere near me. Daleks make me ill – they've ruined my life,' she told the *Daily Record* (6 July 2000) from behind the sofa.

Have fun with fear – create your own new phobia. These 57 have already been done:

Ablutophobia *Fear of washing*
Alektorophobia *Fear of chickens*
Allodoxaphobia *Fear of opinions*
Anginophobia *Fear of sore throats*
Anthophobia *Fear of flowers*
Apotemnophobia *Fear of amputees*
Arachibutyrophobia *Fear of peanut butter*
Automatonophobia *Fear of ventriloquists' dummies*
Bibliophobia *Fear of books*
Bogyphobia *Fear of demons and goblins*
Cacophobia *Fear of ugliness*
Caligynephobia or venustraphobia *Fear of beautiful women*
Cathisophobia or kathisophobia *Fear of sitting down*
Chinophobia *Fear of snow*
Chorophobia *Fear of dancing*
Coitophobia or genophobia *Fear of having sexual intercourse*
Cyberphobia or logizomechanophobia *Fear of computers*
Enosiophobia or enissophobia *Fear of having committed an unpardonable sin*
Eosophobia *Fear of dawn or daylight*
Euphobia *Fear of hearing good news*
Geniophobia *Fear of chins*

Genuphobia *Fear of knees*
Graphophobia *Fear of writing or handwriting*
Hobophobia *Fear of beggars*
Homilophobia *Fear of sermons*
Hygrophobia *Fear of liquids, dampness or moisture*
Kosmikophobia *Fear of cosmic phenomena*
Lacanophobia *Fear of vegetables*
Listophobia *Fear of lists*
Liticaphobia *Fear of lawsuits*
Lutraphobia *Fear of otters*
Macrophobia *Fear of long waits*
Melophobia *Fear or hatred of music*
Metrophobia *Fear or hatred of poetry*
Mnemophobia *Fear of memories*
Myrmecophobia *Fear of ants*
Nomatophobia *Fear of names*
Novercaphobia or pentheraphobia *Fear of mother-in-laws*
Octophobia *Fear of the number eight*
Panophobia or panphobia or pantaphobia *Fear of everything*
Peladophobia *Fear of bald people*
Phobophobia *Fear of fear*
Pluviophobia *Fear of being rained on*
Politicophobia *Fear of politicians*
Proctophobia or rectophobia *Fear of the rectum or rectal diseases*
Pteronophobia *Fear of being tickled by feathers*
Sesquipedalophobia *Fear of long words*
Teratophobia *Fear of giving birth to monsters*
Tremophobia *Fear of trembling*
Venerophobia *Fear of venereal disease*
Vestiphobia *Fear of clothing*
Wiccaphobia *Fear of witches and witchcraft*
Xanthophobia *Fear of colour yellow or word yellow*

Xerophobia *Fear of dryness*
Xylophobia *Fear of wooden objects*
Zeusophobia *Fear of God or gods*
Zoophobia *Fear of animals*

DEATH IS CONTAGIOUS

Celebrity suicides could increase your chance of ending it all – depending on where you learn about them first. A study in *Injury Prevention* (2002, 8; 4: IV30) found that when high-profile political or showbiz personalities kill themselves and become newspaper stories, there is a dramatic increase in the number of copycat suicides.

Televised stories about such people do not have the same effect, nor do plotlines about soap-opera characters, claims the Detroit University research.

COPYCAT CRASHES

Suicide has a bad effect on people's motoring safety, according to a study in the journal *Science* (1977, 196: 1464), which seems to suggest that the best thing to do in your car is switch off the radio news and listen to something jolly. The researchers found that motor vehicle deaths increase just after suicide stories are broadcast by the media.

KNOCKOUT KNOCK-ON

But even if you are in a cheerful mood, if you look like a failed prizefighter you should watch out after high-profile boxing matches for another form of communicable death. A study in the *American Sociology Review*

(1983, 48: 560) shows that murder rates go up after televised fights where there is lots of money offered to the winner.

The increase in your chance of being murdered post-fight is particularly sharp if you bear a physical resemblance to the losing boxer. The greater the amount of publicity given to the story, the higher the subsequent rise in deaths. Perhaps the media should be banned as a health hazard.

BAD STARTS TO LIFE

And from then on, it's all downhill

HAPPY UPBRINGING? WHAT ROTTEN LUCK

Psychologists who followed the lives of 1,216 children assessed in 1922 found that those who were rated as more cheerful and optimistic, and as having a strong sense of humour, died earlier in adult life than those who were less cheerful. Could this help explain why older people seem to moan a lot?

The research flies in the face of the new trend for 'positive psychology' which focuses on boosting happiness rather than alleviating misery as a way of improving your health. Positive psychology is based on findings such as a Yale University psychologists' study of 660 volunteers aged 50 and above, which found that thinking positively about ageing may add an average of seven-and-a-half years to your life. The team, led by Dr Becca Levy, suggests in the *Journal of Personality and Social Psychology* (2002, 83; 2: 261) that having an optimistic attitude can bolster the will to live, although they admit they can't explain it fully.

But that would not impress the cheerful-child researchers from the University of California, the State University of New York Medical School and La Sierra University. They say the happy youngsters they followed 'grew up to be more likely to die in any given year but not more likely to die of any particular cause'.

The researchers found that the cheerful kids grew up more likely to drink, smoke and take risks, possibly because their optimism makes the dangers appear smaller to them – 'Hey, but it might be a *friendly* shark,' or that old classic, 'Go on, have a smoke, you might get run over by a bus tomorrow, har har.' But still the scientists add: 'These behaviours cannot fully explain their relatively early deaths.'

The report, in *Personality and Social Psychology Bulletin* (2002, 28: 1155), concludes, 'Although optimism and positive emotions have been shown to have positive effects when people are faced with short-term crisis, the long-term effects of cheerfulness are more complex and seem not entirely positive.' If there is a bright side to this report, it seems you are better off not looking for it.

WAR? BRUTALITY? BLAME THE PARENTS

Blame your upbringing for your controlling, tyrannical tendencies. Were it not for bad parenting, the world could have been spared the likes of Saddam Hussein, Hitler, Stalin and Idi Amin, according to the American war psychologist Jerome Frank.

Frank, an emeritus professor of psychiatry at Johns Hopkins Medical School, argues that the modern age's worst tyrants shared 'strikingly similar' brutal formative years. He writes in *Medicine and War* (March 1994) that Hussein's early childhood was dominated by a brutal stepfather who raised him in abject squalor. As a child, Hussein displayed typical symptoms of early abuse, being 'angry, suspicious, guarded and self-centred'.

His mother was remarkably aggressive. She once reportedly screamed at a doctor, 'You son of a bitch, if my daughter dies I will erect your gallows outside the hospital and hang you.' The doctor fainted.

The Stalins were also unpopular neighbours, writes Frank. Joseph Stalin's father, a violent drunk who often subjected him to savage and undeserved beatings, died in a bar-room brawl. His mother thrashed young Joseph regularly. Frank says that as an adult, Stalin became preoccupied with beatings as a way of securing confessions. He was also noted for his unfailing memory for insult and injury.

Idi Amin and Adolf Hitler's families also merited the intervention of social services, the professor says. Amin's parents split before he was born, and he may never have known his father. While he was a child, his mother went with soldiers and practised witchcraft.

Then there was Hitler, whose upbringing featured a self-perpetuating cycle of violence. His remote, authoritarian father was a harsh disciplinarian who was himself brutalized in childhood.

Professor Frank, the author of *Sanity and Survival in the Nuclear Age*, says all four leaders grew up believing violence an appropriate means of resolving arguments, and may have developed extreme bloodthirstiness as a way of coping with the 'death anxiety' instilled by their childhood terrors. Poor lambs.

PRENATAL DELINQUENTS

Another reason to blame your mother: pregnant women who smoke are four times more likely to have delinquent sons, claim Chicago University researchers. They say their study of 177 children shows that mums who smoke more than ten a day put their boys at far greater risk of **conduct disorder**

– the modern clinical term for lying, bullying, stealing and vandalism.

Maternal smoking may inhibit development in the unborn baby's brain so it is less able to produce the feelgood drug, serotonin, and this may lead to thrill-seeking behaviours, suggest the child-development experts in the American Medical Association's *Archives of General Psychiatry* (1997, 54; 7: 670).

On the other hand, psychologists at Illinois–Chicago University say the link could be down to good old-fashioned heredity. They report in *Addictive Behaviour* (2004, 29; 2: 273) that mothers who smoke during pregnancy are markedly more likely to have been delinquents themselves. Like mother, like son.

IS YOUR DREAD FATE IN YOUR PALM?

Palmistry might seem an arrant load of fairground nonsense, but our fingerprints and palms do seem to be accurate predictors of future health fortunes, argue researchers in the *British Medical Journal* (1993, 307; 6901: 405).

Their study followed up 139 babies born around 50 years ago in Preston, Lancashire, UK, whose birth weight, placental weight, head circumference and length at birth were recorded. Then they looked at the subjects' fingerprints and palm-prints, to see if they had any whorls – patterns formed when the prints on the fingerprints go beyond the usual arches or loops and become complete circles.

The 93 men and women with a whorl pattern on one or more fingers had significantly higher blood pressure than the 46 people who did not have whorls. Whorls on the right hand were more strongly linked to high pressure than whorls on the left.

The researchers believe that this is because people who are thin at birth are apparently more likely to have whorls on their hands. They also have a higher risk of blood-pressure problems, possibly due to foetal undernutrition. Fingerprint patterns are, the researchers say, accurate markers for patterns for foetal growth – rather like rings in trees.

NO, NO – IT'S YOUR EAR

That fleshy protuberance on the left of your head could hold vital clues to your chances of a heart attack. Doctors examining cadavers have noticed over the years that people killed by cardiac trouble seem much more likely to have a diagonal crease on their left ear lobe. That's right, get a mirror and check.

Researchers at St Thomas' Hospital speculated in the 1980s that the left ear is linked with the heart when a foetus is growing in the womb, and may show related abnormalities by having a crease.

Dr Robert Superko goes further in his 2004 book *Before the Heart Attacks*, claiming you need to look for a 45-degree diagonal crease on both ears. The co-founder of California's Berkeley HeartLab says the crease points upwards towards your eyebrows, and suggests, 'since both heart disease and ear creases are inherited, we think that these genes are somehow bundled together ... this ear crease does act as an informal predictive marker for increased risk.'

Not everyone is convinced. The textbook *Cardiac Diseases*, published by Harcourt International, says the presence of a diagonal earlobe crease is linked to heart attacks in some studies, but not in others. It says the association may be flawed because people get more ear creases the older they get.

Hairy ears could be a bad omen, though. The Harcourt authors add that the presence of hair in the ear-canal has also been linked with increased risk of coronary disease.

After you have given up trying to hold the mirror so you can see inside your ear, check your iris. Is there a white ring around it? It's called the arcus senilis and, according to Superko, this is another sign that you could be about to keel over with cardiac trouble.

LIFE GIVES YOU THE FINGER

Now look at your hand again. Scientists at Liverpool University claim that the ratio of finger length to body height can indicate if a man is liable to suffer depression.

Their study of 102 men and women in *Evolution and Human Behaviour* (1999, 20: 203) concludes that the longer a man's fingers are relative to his height, the more likely he is to get the blues. The strongest single indicator is the relative length of his wedding-ring finger.

The study suggests that low levels of prenatal testosterone, produced from the eighth week of pregnancy, rather than day-by-day testosterone levels in adults, is responsible. Dr John Manning of Liverpool University School of Biological Sciences says, 'Foetal testosterone plays a key role in the development of the male genital system. It also impacts on the development of fingers and thumbs, and the central nervous system.

'Men who experienced high concentrations of foetal testosterone have relatively long fingers – in particular, fourth digits which are longer than their second digits. Conversely, men who experienced low concentrations of foetal testosterone have shorter fourth digits than their second digits.'

The researchers divided digit length by height, to take account of the fact that taller men tend to have longer limbs, fingers and feet.

PINKIE PATERNITY

This is not the first time Dr Manning has identified a hidden significance of finger length. In 1998 he established a link between the relative length of women's ring fingers and their fertility levels: women with shorter ring fingers than forefingers tend to have high fertility. Conversely, men with relatively long ring fingers are more likely to have high fertility.

The doctor went on to investigate a possible association between risk of heart attack and second-to-fourth digit ratio. He also claims the ratio may also hold clues about your chances of autism, dyslexia, migraine, stammering and breast cancer.

SHORT-CHANGED

Here's something else to worry about that you can't alter – your height. You are apparently cursed for life if you grow slowly in the first 12 months after birth. This won't just affect your blood pressure – it will also lower your income, believes a researcher at the University of Southampton.

Professor David Barker says his results hold true regardless of family, class or poverty, and that this suggests that slow infant growth may be accompanied by impaired brain development.

The University of Southampton researcher revealed his findings at the Second World Congress on the Fetal Origins of Adult Disease, saying, 'biological processes linked to poor growth in infancy lead to lifelong impairment of cognitive function with consequent lower occupational status and income.' In layman's terms, it means being short is likely to leave you dumb, common and poor.

'Although children who are short at any age up to puberty tend to do less well educationally and have lower incomes in later life, most of the action is in the first year,' he adds.

Dr Barker, the author of *The Best Start in Life*, has pioneered research into how adult diseases begin in the womb, based on a study of 4,630 men born in Helsinki between 1934 and 1944. Research from his group has also shown that low infant growth is also linked to later risk of death from heart disease and type 2 diabetes, as well as less impressive bank accounts.

'There are two organs that are not complete when the baby's born – one of them is the brain. And brain development between birth and one is known to be important,' he says. 'The liver is also not complete, and the liver sets how the body handles cholesterol which is probably the link with heart disease.

'Weight at one year in boys predicts their cognitive function. Boys who grow better between birth and one have better educational achievements and they make more money when they're 50,' he says.

'Since, in a democratic society, income is a test of cognitive function among other things, this is rather a striking demonstration of the critical period of growth between birth and one year.'

SPEAK UPWARDS

Being afflicted by small babyhood is also behind Swedish doctors' claim that short people are more likely to go deaf in old age. Their study of 479 men, reported in the *British Medical Journal* (2002, 327; 7425: 1199), led them to conclude that age-related disorders such as hearing loss happen earlier if you are born with low levels of human growth hormone.

ON THE OTHER HAND ...

Being tall can kill. A Bristol University study in the *Journal of Epidemiology and Community Health* (2000, 54; 2: 97) warns that loftiness is associated with an increased risk of dying from some cancers, particularly blood, colon and rectal cancers and, for men, prostate cancer.

And tall men are more likely than shorties to commit suicide, an American university study found. Men shorter than 5ft 6in are particularly less prone to self-destruct, says the sociologist Dr Steven Stack, in the *Journal of Social Psychology* (1996, 136; 2: 255).

He says this is because diminutive chaps have to develop better psychological self-defence skills when young to compensate for their lack of stature – such as the ability to tell jokes in the playground, and to hold their breath when their head is being pushed down the loo.

Being really tall is apparently the worst health risk, which surely explains how very few lanky octogenarians one sees on the streets. Thomas Samaras, an American scientist, reported the risk in the *Bulletin of the World Health Organization* (1992, 70; 2: 259). He studied 3,600 baseball players and found a direct relationship between height and life expectancy. 'As the men got taller, their average age at death dropped,' he says. 'It came out to be about one year less life expectancy per inch.'

Perhaps it is about time someone researched the manifold health perils of being merely average. 'Non-remarkable height syndrome'? Surely it must exist.

SLAP ATTACK

Men who go bald early in their lives should worry less about their receding youth – and more about their increased chance of a heart attack.

A long-term study of men in Framingham, Massachusetts, found that men who develop 'monk's pate' pattern baldness – where hair is lost from the crown as well as the front – before they reach 55, have an increased risk of heart problems.

The researchers report in the *Journal of the American Medical Association* (1993, 269; 8: 1035) that they suspect it is linked to dihydrotestosterone (DHT). People with lots of DHT receptors in their scalp tend to go bald early. There are also DHT receptors in other organs, including the heart and liver, where it seems they can also cause problems if they are over-stimulated. Scientists at Boston University say that men who develop monk's pate hair loss under the age of 55 are particularly at risk.

You could always try to avert this problem by drinking heavily (lawyer's note – don't). Dr Hugh Rushton, a fellow of Britain's Institute of Trichologists and an authority on hair loss, says alcohol binges protect against baldness. Binge drinkers have livers that are so damaged that they are no longer capable of properly processing the testosterone that lies at the root of the baldness/heart-attack problem.

'If you force a man to drink too much alcohol, it is very unlikely he will lose his hair,' claims Dr Rushton. 'If you wander down London's Strand, you will see the evidence. How many of the alcoholics are ever bald?'

CARDIAC CLOSE SHAVE

Men who do not shave every day are more than three times as likely to suffer a stroke than those who do, a 20-year study indicates. Bristol University researchers asked 2,438 men from Caerphilly, South Wales, how often they needed to lather up. Their susceptibility to heart disease and strokes was then monitored over a 20-year period.

The study found that those who do not shave every day are also more likely to smoke, less likely to be married and more likely to do manual work, says the report in the *American Journal of Epidemiology* (2003, 158; 11: 1123). But even after adjusting their health risks for these factors, the seldom-shavers were reportedly up to 70 per cent more likely to suffer strokes and more likely to die prematurely from any cause.

✝

REDUNDANT DISEASES

Some social scourges just seem to disappear

RAILWAY SPINE

Along with the new-fangled railways of the Victorian era came a whole new-fangled illness: railway spine. People caught up in the era's frequent rail accidents suffered a wide array of symptoms including 'obscure affections of the brain and spinal cord'. Often these only appeared a long time after the accident.

In many cases such symptoms were seen in patients who had no detectable injury or neurological damage. Others experienced symptoms that were far more serious than one would expect from their modest injuries. Perhaps this was because there were lawyers involved.

Railway spine was usually associated with back pain, other chronic pain and anxiety – and it was often linked to a compensation claim for damages. The 1923 *Illustrated Family Doctor*, published by the *London Household Encyclopaedia*, says, 'The nervous disorders that may follow a railway collision or any similar accident are usually of a hysterical nature. The fact that the patient often recovers very quickly after his claim for compensation has been finally dealt with does not necessarily imply malingering.'

When the courts began to treat sufferers with increasing scepticism, railway spine largely disappeared from the medical textbooks. Some experts, however, say we can thank railway spine – and its psychosomatic origins – for the birth of American psychotherapy.

NEURASTHENIA

When neurasthenia appeared in the Victorian era, thousands of women took to their beds with a host of vague exhaustion-related symptoms. But around the Second World War, the condition simply disappeared. George Somerville, the deputy superintendent of the West Ham Mental Hospital in 1930, described the condition – and the 'neurotics' who suffered it – in *The Hygiene of Life and Safer Motherhood* manual's special *Personal Supplement* – the bit that women hid in the back of the wardrobe.

'This nervous illness is shown by signs of exhaustion not only of mind but of body. Most often the woman has suffered from a state of irritable nerves for some prolonged period before she decides she is really ill. The symptoms complained of are many. Most characteristically there is an "always tired" feeling. All effort, physical or mental, is painful.'

Somerville, not a man given to wild displays of compassion, adds: 'The neurasthenic woman finds it impossible to concentrate, and is unduly self-centred and excessively concerned with her bodily health. She has an acute sense of her incapacity and, although she knows that most of her fears are groundless, she is unable to make the effort to get rid of them. Hence it is of little value to tell the nervous woman to "buck up" or "get well". What is required is to teach her how to make the effort to overcome her troubles.

'The nervous illnesses of women respond well to treatment and the sooner the unhappy victims seek expert advice, the sooner and more completely will they free themselves from the tyranny of "nerves" and return to their normal health.'

What happened to neurasthenia? Some commentators say it got rebranded: critics of ME or chronic fatigue syndrome claim it is merely neurasthenia under a new name. The person with ME often has disabling fatigue, muscle pain, flu-like malaise, loss of concentration and short-term memory, sensitivity to light and noise, and sometimes depression and mood swings. It does all sound rather familiar.

BROW AGUE

This persistent ache behind one eye could prove extremely dangerous, warned Johnson Walsham in 1887. No ordinary ache this; it was 'associated with malaria' and could be very painful and be accompanied by twitches. It might also be caused by mouth disease or sinus problems. But failure to remedy it could 'unhinge the patient's mind, disposing them towards thoughts of suicide'.

Surgery could fix it, says Johnson in *Surgery, Its Theory and Practice*. 'This is carried out by exposing the nerve above the orbit and raising it on a hook. The hook then draws out the nerve, or it can be rolled over the closed jaws of a pair of forceps. This approach appears singularly successful, as patients rarely return for a further procedure.'

DEATH BY TEETHING

Teething nowadays is considered an inconvenience for babies and parents alike. But historically, the condition has aroused deep fear and apprehension. Hippocrates warned: 'Teething children suffer from itching of the gums, fever, convulsions, diarrhoea.' And it has even been thought lethal. Fatal teething was listed frequently in early Utah death records.

A physician named Arbuthnot wrote in 1732, 'Above one-tenth part of all children die in teething (some of them from gangrene).' As recently as 1979, an English child's death was recorded as 'teething convulsions'.

The *Western Journal of Medicine* (1991, 155; 6: 658) quotes a 1905 American home health-care book saying, 'A very common cause of diseases of the stomach and bowels, and also of convulsions in children, is to be found in the hardening or induration of the gums at the time of teething, and this blunder of nature's ought to be promptly remedied whenever the gums in infants at the time of the first dentition are found to be red, swollen, and hot to the touch.'

What actually caused the Utah deaths remains a mystery. From 1847 to 1881, 521 babies' deaths were attributed to teething or related conditions. The number of cases increased gradually each year until 1866, when they jumped significantly. The vast majority of cases occurred from August to December. The level remained relatively high for several more years. Then, almost as quickly, the number of 'teething deaths' fell and virtually disappeared.

Some experts suggest that the actual cause of death was most likely sudden infant death syndrome (Sids), but the average age for 'teething deaths' was 13 months. Most studies find Sids usually occurs before six months.

FLOATING KIDNEYS

Doctors don't like to say they don't know what's wrong with you. So sometimes they will invent an answer. One of their past creations was the floating kidney. Medics actually believed that patients' vague symptoms were caused by gravity pulling the kidney down.

The cure? Obvious: fix the kidney in place by putting a stitch through its wall and hitching it up to some nearby muscle. In the 1920s and 1930s such operations were common, averaging 20 a year at the Glasgow Royal Infirmary alone. Then quite suddenly it went out of fashion.

NYMPHOMANIA

This was originally a vague term stuck on to any female sexual desire thought excessive or troublesome. It was, however, defined as a definite mental illness in 19th-century asylums, where one cure was to attach leeches to sufferers' vaginas. Historians now consider nymphomania part of a Victorian obsession with controlling women's self-expression. But 'exaggerated sexual craving in women' continued to trouble doctors until the end of the 20th century.

In 1942, Edward Podolsky MD's *Modern Sex Manual* lamented that, 'For many years the treatment and management of exaggerated sexual craving in women has been a problem which many physicians and psychiatrists have had to face in daily consultation. Frankly there was actually very little that could be done.'

Podolsky warned that many women suddenly develop increased sexual desire during the menopause. The danger sign (apart of course from an overflowing collection of frothy lingerie) was 'a sudden increase in weight, which is directly related to the sexual craving'. How ironic. Or perhaps some men suddenly found their expanding wives' desires to be excessive.

The doctor thought the sex urge was controlled in women by the pituitary gland at the base of the skull, and that problems began when this became overactive. There was, however, hope, he said: 'With startling advances in female hormonology this problem is well on the way toward solution. The new remedy is, strangely enough, the male sex hormone, or testosterone propionate. It is injected once every two days. In most cases, relief is obtained within three weeks or a month. In some cases there is a recurrence of the morbid sex craving.'

Alternatives were few: 'Mental treatment has been tried, but simply telling a woman to exert some willpower to control her abnormal sex craving is not enough,' Podolsky said. The craving could be sublimated, though: 'Lecturing, travelling, writing and doing other work which requires physical and emotional expenditure of energy has often been found effective in nullifying unusually strong sexual desire.'

Nymphomania was still defined as a sexual deviation in 1951, in America's first official attempt to categorize psychiatric illness: the *Diagnostic and Statistical Manual of Mental Disorders*. It was still there in 1980, described as 'a psychosexual disorder'. Nymphomania only disappeared from the manual in the 1990s.

Nowadays the only female libido 'problem', as recently defined by drug companies keen to sell sexual stimulants to the fairer gender, is **female sexual**

dysfunction, or FSD. This is characterized by an apparent 'lack of desire'. How times change.

OUT OF THE ARC

Nineteenth-century physicians could get a bit too holistic. Many believed that one cause of illness was the **reflex-arc theory**. This proposed that every organ in the body could influence, by reflex, every other organ, no matter how far away. The Toronto University historian, Edward Shorter, says that because most psychosomatic patients were women, the most popular reflex-arc procedure was to remove the uterus. The poor patients, with implicit faith in their doctors, suffered gladly, he laments in his book, *From Paralysis to Fatigue*.

FOCAL SEPSIS

In the early part of the 20th century, focal sepsis, or localized infection, usually of the teeth, was blamed for many illnesses, including rheumatism, gastritis, sclerosis, pernicious anaemia and so on.

The solution: total dental extraction. All your teeth. Out.

While this was a boon for the dental prosthetics industry, it didn't do much for the poor toothless people diagnosed with focal sepsis – whose illnesses were in fact caused by a wide variety of conditions. One by one, the proper causes of the diseases were identified – pernicious anaemia, for example, was found to be caused by a deficiency of vitamin B12.

Focal sepsis quietly slinked out of medical textbooks.

CLERGYMAN'S THROAT

The 1923 *Illustrated Family Doctor*, published by the *London Household Encyclopaedia*, describes this as, 'A chronic inflammation of the structures at the back of the throat, thus called on account of its being caused to a large extent by an overuse or misuse of the voice. The mucous membrane at the back of the throat is dotted with little dark red elevations varying in size from a pinhead to a pea, or even larger in some cases.

'A visit to a spa possessing laxative waters is often beneficial. The granules at the back of the throat should be destroyed by galvano-cautery or in some other way.' Ouch.

DANCING PLAGUE

Mass outbreaks of imagined illnesses did not only arrive with the industrial revolution. From the 13th to the 16th centuries in Europe, large populations became afflicted by the dancing plague – frenzied dancing in which thousands of people became exhausted, often to the point of death.

Dancing plague spread through Holland, Germany and France over three centuries. It was characterized by an uncontrollable impulse to dance and a morbid love of music, and mostly affected women and poor people. Although it was primarily confined to continental Europe, there was also recorded an outbreak of 'the Leaping Ague' in Scotland, and other frenzies in Abyssinia and Madagascar.

At the time, the plague was commonly blamed on demonic possession resulting from invalid baptisms by a corrupt clergy. While its exact cause remains a mystery, it is commonly thought to have been a mass-hysterical response to the general misery of life in the grim Middle Ages, with its famines, mass deaths, pestilences and epidemics. The idea that it was a form of social hysteria is supported by the fact that people only had to see or hear another person dancing to become afflicted themselves.

By the mid-19th century, dancing plague had disappeared. But it was not forgotten. Physicians' suspicion of dancing's anarchic soul re-emerged in the journal, *Industrial Medical Surgery* (1960, 29: 51), where the authors warned that dancing plague had re-emerged in the 20th century in the demonic form of rock'n'roll.

Perhaps it has not ended there. In 1995, epidemiologists in Newcastle upon Tyne and Fife, Scotland, suggested in *Public Health* (1995, 111: 201) that 'popular crazes such as breakdancing and raves associated with the drug ecstasy may be the modern-day equivalents. They may be a cultural response to adversity.'

TRY SUING FOR THESE

Defunct occupational illnesses:
Chauffeur's knee
Chimney sweeper's scrotum
Coal miner's nystagmus
Factory fever
Hatter's shakes
Matchmaker's phossy jaw
Painters' colic

Telegrapher's cramp
Woolsorter's disease

Source: *Diseases of Unusual Occupations: An Historical Perspective,*
Occupational Medicine: State of the Art Reviews (1992, 7; 3:
369–384)

SPORT AND LEISURE

Did you really think you'd be safe at playtime?

GOLFBALL LIVER

Licking your balls might possibly lower your handicap, but it can also give you hepatitis.

Many golf players believe licking the ball can increase its speed in the air. That may be superstitious tosh, but doctors have discovered a definite consequence – golfball liver. They found the condition in a 65-year-old retired engineer who developed abdominal pain and lethargy while playing golf in Ireland.

The man, who played golf every day, was thought after a medical examination to have hepatitis, but his doctors could not decide how he acquired the liver disease. Then it emerged he habitually licked his golf ball clean to make it travel faster, even though signs at the golf course warned of the groundkeepers' widespread use of the weedkiller 2,4-Dichlorophenoxyacetic acid – also known as Agent Orange.

The doctors diagnosed golfball liver, caused by the toxic weedkiller he had been swallowing. The patient stopped his golfball licking and his symptoms cleared up. But then, sceptical of the medical theory, he started doing it again and landed back at hospital.

Dr Connor Burke from James Connolly Memorial Hospital, Dublin, and colleagues, wrote in the journal *Gut* (1997, 40; 5: 687), 'Our patient finally accepted his diagnosis of golfball liver. He plays golf regularly, carries a damp cloth to clean his golf ball and remains well, to date, with normal liver function tests five years after his acute presentation.

'We suggest that golfball liver is a definite clinical entity and that golfers should beware.'

BOLT FROM THE GREEN

Men are more than four times more likely than women to be struck by lightning, according to *Canadian Geographic* magazine (January 2000). Could this be because they are more likely to play golf?

Golfers are especially at risk because they spend so much time on wide-open courses during the summer, when lightning is most common. The American National Lightning Safety Institute (NLSI) says people on golf courses account for about 5 per cent of lightning deaths and injuries each year in the United States.

The most famous incident was during the Western Open golf championship in Chicago on 27 June 1975. The champion player Lee Trevino was sitting on the edge of a green by a lake waiting for a shower to pass when lightning threw him into the air. He was rushed to hospital where four burn marks were left on his shoulder where the lightning had left his body. Though his injured back gave him pain for several years he returned to form.

During the past 30 years, lightning has killed an average of 73 people and injured hundreds each year in the United States, says the US National Weather

Service. If you are out on the golf course, the NLSI has a simple lightning rule: if you can see it, flee it. The NLSI says to seek shelter when lightning is within six miles of you. God doesn't shout 'Fore!'

PENIS SUBSTITUTE?

Men who ride motorcycles to impress women may be in for an unpleasant surprise. French accident-and-emergency unit researchers have discovered worrying levels of phallic injuries among Gallic bikers.

These are caused by riders smacking crotch-first into their petrol tanks when their bikes hit an obstacle. The resulting haemorrhages, ruptures and lesions are enough to stop motorcyclists ever showing a perfect wheelie to the girls again. The doctors from Nice politely warn in *Injury* (1994, 25; 4: 223), 'The accident can have after-effects that jeopardize the social and family life of the patients.'

Similar damage is reported by doctors in the *Journal of Trauma* (2002, 53; 4: 806) who have christened it **motor scooter handlebar syndrome**. But there is a bright side. Pathologists from Izumo, Japan, say it can help in the legally important task of finding out who was in control, and who was riding pillion when both die in a crash. Easy, they say in the *American Journal of Forensic Medical Pathology* (1990, 11; 3: 190): the pillion is the one without the lacerated crotch.

MOVING-GOALPOST MURDER

Look out for that crossbar. Twenty-seven people were killed or injured by falling soccer goalposts between 1979 and 1993 in America alone, a nation not known for being soccer mad, reports the *Morbidity and Mortality Weekly Report* (1994, 43; 9: 153).

GOALKEEPER'S FINGER

Short, married, amateur goalie? Take care of your wedding finger.

The plastic surgery unit at Canniesburn Hospital, Glasgow, reports in the *Journal of Hand Surgery* (1994, 19; 4: 459) of three goalkeepers who lost their ring fingers in remarkably similar accidents while setting up their nets.

In each instance, the goalkeeper was trying to attach the nets to the goalposts by jumping up with the netting in his hand while trying to place it over the crossbar hooks. The wedding rings on the goalies' fingers got hooked instead – and there they hung, until they sustained what medical professionals call a degloving injury: the skin of the finger is entirely pulled off and the finger has to be amputated.

The writers warn that amateur footballers are proven to be more prone to the injury than their professional counterparts. Professionals do not have to set up their own nets. More importantly, all the injured goalies were less than 1.68m tall – so they had to jump to reach the crossbar. Lessons? Go professional, wear gloves, stay single and never be a short goalie.

Also from the annals of sports research comes **spinner's finger**; if you play a lot of cricket you are likely to develop callouses on your bowling fingers. These tend to crack, and the resulting condition is known as spinner's finger.

Then there is also **paddler's palsy**, identified in the *New England Journal of Medicine*, (1996, 334; 2: 125), by Dr C. Harker Rhodes. You can suddenly experience dramatic loss of strength in your hands after kayaking, caused by energetic stretching of the shoulders while paddling about.

The *New England Journal of Medicine* has a habit of publishing physicians' reports of leisure-activity injuries:

There's:

- **Space Invaders wrist**
- Also **cuber's thumb**, *caused by obsessive wrestling with a* Rubik's Cube
- *In similar vein, there is* **GameBox thumb**
- *And the equally self-explanatory* **knitter's finger**
- *And then there is* **slot-machine tendonitis** *– which must be closely related to* **slot-machine sprain**: *Richard Neiman MD, of the University of California, reveals 'an affliction rarely seen by physicians practising outside of easy driving distance of gambling casinos'.*

He tells of two patients who complained of painful right shoulders – and no apparent cause – until they said they had both spent the previous weekend on the one-armed bandits. Like many addicts, they had been playing hard and fast.

'Reproduction of the movement required to play slot machines produced excruciating pain,' Neiman says in the *New England Journal of Medicine* (1981, 304; 22: 1368). Steroids could be injected to relieve the pain but, he writes, 'continued trauma after steroid therapy may result in rupture of the tendon.'

His solution: 'Rest – or win a jackpot early.'

SCUBA-DIVING DEMENTIA

If you have joined the craze for amateur scuba diving, then be wary. It may cause bends-type brain injuries without anyone even noticing.

Neuro-radiologists who studied 50 experienced amateur divers for a *Lancet* report (1995, 345; 8962: 1403) found that they had eight times the number of small brain injuries compared with counterparts who engaged in other sports. While the individual injuries to blood vessels in the brain would not be significant, they may have a cumulative effect, the report says.

The German researchers say that the injuries, which can be caused by getting the classic diver's bends by resurfacing too quickly and getting nitrogen bubbles in the blood, have been found to cause depression, memory loss and lower IQ in professional divers.

BICYCLIST'S VULVA

Mind that vicious cycle: Belgian doctors warn that keen women riders can develop this feminine form of saddle-soreness, which rather speaks for itself.

They report in the *British Medical Journal* (2002, 325; 7356: 138) the cases of six women, aged from 21 to 38, who suffered a one-sided swelling of their labia after spending several years cycling on average 462.5km a week – which in any normal terms could be considered:

A: *Excessive*
B: *Probably indicative of poor sex life.*

It was not the fault of the type of shorts worn, or the cleanliness of each woman's perineum (that bit 'twixt front bottom and back bottom), which the doctors, based at Brugmann University Hospital, Brussels, said were all 'optimum'. But all six women regularly had saddle-related rashes, chronic inflammation of the saddle area, and five had scars, perineal chafing and nodules.

Cycling seems to damage the body's mechanism for moving fluid around – the lymphatic system – in the upper thighs, the doctors warn. They conclude that this had caused the women's swellings. They suggest keen pedallers put their feet up when resting, to aid lymphatic drainage.

The Victorians may have discovered this first. The Cycle Touring Club of Great Britain in the late 1800s refused to allow women's racing, on grounds of female physiology, for several decades.

PEDALLER'S PENIS

Men can be at risk as well. Trondheim doctors studied 260 male cycle racers after a competition that spanned 540km, and found many suffered embarrassing problems caused by nerve entrapment. The cyclists developed the male anatomical equivalent of a slow puncture.

Thirteen per cent of them suffered impotence for at least a week after the race and 21 per cent suffered cycling-related penile numbness. In some cyclists, the symptoms lasted for up to eight months, the Norwegian researchers report in *Acta Neurology Scandinavia* (1997, 95; 4: 233).

PUSHBIKE PROSTATE

The cycle of misery does not stop there: Kevin O'Brien, of the Southern California Permanente Medical Group, reports how three men turned up at his surgery in the space of a month with problems peeing – abrupt need to go, dribbling, feeble wee – all common symptoms of prostate trouble. But no, instead it was pushbike prostate.

'Each patient was able to relate the onset of symptoms either to the purchase of a ten-speed bicycle or an exercise bike,' he says. The patients were warned of the danger of putting all their weight on their perineum – i.e. sitting on a thin bike saddle. The doctor reports that 'voiding habits returned to normal after either discontinuation of cycling or modification of the seat.'

But how many men, Dr O'Brien wonders in the *New England Journal of Medicine* (28 May 1981), have been subjected to risky prostate surgery when all they needed was to get off their bikes?

UNICYCLIST'S SCIATICA

In the light of this, it is no surprise to learn of unicyclist's sciatica – caused by the rider putting all their weight upon the perineum. This was reported by Steven Gold of Boston University School of Medicine.

Symptoms include moderate nerve pain down the buttocks and thighs, and a burning sensation upon peeing. 'It is evident that the hazards of unicycle riding go beyond the obvious orthopaedic considerations (e.g. a broken neck),' he says in the *New England Journal of Medicine* (1981, 305; 4: 231).

SLAM-DUNK DEATH

A simple game of garage-wall basketball could end in injury or worse. The Royal Australian Institute of Architects has warned of the dangers of home basketball hoops after three deaths. The problem? It's the modern craze for slam-dunking.

Household walls are not built to take the force of a well-slammed dunk, where you swing on the hoop and score mightily. Hapless back-yard ballplayers are causing walls to collapse, bringing tons of lethal masonry down on top of them, warn the experts in Queensland's *Sunday Mail* (23 February 2003).

SNOWMOBILER'S HAEMATURIA

Winter sports fan? You risk a worrying condition if you insist on racing around with a full bladder, warns the *Canadian Medical Association Journal* (2003, 168; 6: 670). It reports a case of haematuria – that's passing urine with lots of blood in it – in March 1983, after a patient was examined for mystery symptoms that were not explained by the usual diagnoses of sexual infection, or prostate or abdominal trouble.

Then the patient revealed he was a keen snowmobiler, and his doctor, Malvinder Parmar (who earlier brought us Tight Trousers Syndrome and Telephone Stroke), decided that this was the cause of the patient's troubles. He says the 'repetitive impact of the man's partially filled bladder against the bladder base during each thrust caused bladder irritation, leading to transient gross haematuria.'

Parmar speculates that, 'Because snowmobiling is a common recreational activity, this association may be under-recognized.'

FAIRGROUND STROKE

Roller-coasters can blow your mind. The French doctor Valerie Biousse and colleagues tell of a 31-year-old woman dance teacher who suffered a mild stroke caused by damage to her left vertebral artery. She had no history of troubles before admitting herself to l'Hopital Saint-Antoine, Paris, but said her symptoms first appeared two days after going on the Space Mountain roller-coaster in Disneyland Paris. 'The delay of 48 hours between the onset of pain and the ride on the roller-coaster makes it likely that the roller-coaster was responsible,' says the report in the *Lancet* (1995, 346; 8977: 767). Vertebral artery damage 'is a frequent cause of stroke in young adults', it adds.

'They are often associated with indirect trauma or torsion of the neck. The acceleration and abrupt changes of direction on the roller-coaster might have induced uncontrolled rotation of the head ... as observed in some car-crash casualties.'

That might sound like a one-off, but medics are keen to report that it's not all fun at the fair. Minneapolis doctors at the Hennepin County Medical Center report in the *Annals of Emergency Medicine* (2002, 39; 1: 65) that between 1979 and 1999 roller-coaster rides have been blamed in America for four cases of brain bruising, six burst arteries, three haemorrhages and one stroke.

And doctors at the l'Hopital Jean Verdier, Bondy, France, found six cases of severe injuries after roller-coaster rides, including damaged veins in the brain and haemorrhaging, they report in *Presse Medicin* (2000, 29; 4: 175). Though such roller-coaster induced brain injuries 'are highly uncommon', they can leave victims disabled or dead, they warn.

FUNFAIR MIGRAINE

Roller-coasters can also leave you with a blinding headache. Los Angeles doctors record how they examined a 28-year-old woman complaining of severe headaches, sleep problems, memory problems and irritability two months after a violent roller-coaster ride. In the journal *Headache* (2000, 40; 9: 745), they write how they diagnosed her with post-traumatic migraine, and blamed 'the many short but significant brain insults delivered during the roller-coaster ride as a critical factor'.

ROLLERBLINDNESS

Fairground rides can make you go temporarily blind, too. Ophthalmologists at the Manchester Royal Eye Hospital report how a short period of intensive roller-coaster rides left a 19-year-old woman with reduced vision in one eye. They found damage to an artery in her retina, but were happy to report that her focus returned 'after a period of avoidance of roller-coaster rides' in the *American Journal of Ophthalmology* (2000, 130; 4: 527).

ROLLER-COASTER LOVE

Those are not the only dangers of thrill-a-minute rides. They can also send you blindly in love, by making you become amorously fixated on complete strangers. This warning on the dangers of inappropriate sexual liaisons caused by fairgrounds comes courtesy of psychologists at the University of Texas at Austin, who experimented on passers-by as they were about to get on or off a roller-coaster.

They showed the fair-goers a photograph of an average-looking member of the opposite sex and asked them to rate the pictured person's attractive-ness and date-worthiness. People riding the roller-coaster alone were far more likely to think the person in the photograph sexy if they were shown it after they had finished the ride than before they got on it, the researchers say in the *Archives of Sexual Behaviour* (2003, 32; 6: 537).

Why? The shrinks say that it is evidence of 'exci-tation transfer' theory, where people are more likely to be romantically aroused in thrilling or perilous cir-cumstances. We see it happen in adventure films all the time – but you really should be very careful about falling in love with anyone you meet at a fairground. 'This is my new girlfriend. She has a beautiful person-ality, underneath that beard.'

LETHAL STRIKE-OUT

Strike one: young athletes, be wary – you are at risk of instant sudden death caused by getting smacked so hard in the chest that it stops your heart. Being struck by a baseball travelling at 40mph is particularly dead-ly, reports *Progress in Biophysical Molecular Biology* (2003, 82; 1–3: 175).

The impact causes the heart to go into ventricu-lar fibrillation, causing a 'significant percentage of deaths on the athletics field,' say cardiac experts at Tufts University School of Medicine, Boston. They add that the medical name for this lethal condition is *com-motio cordis*, and add, 'Sudden death is instantaneous or preceded by several seconds of light-headedness after the chest-wall blow.' The scientists fired base-balls at a hapless young pig (producing a sound that, once heard, is never forgotten), and discovered that any ball travelling at 30mph or more could cause lethal heart trouble. They concluded that 40mph is the most lethal speed. Any faster or slower was significantly less dangerous.

TWO, FOUR, SIX, EIGHT: CHEERLEADING CAN DEVASTATE

Few sporting activities sound less perilous than prancing around with a pair of pom-poms and a short skirt – but even cheerleading can cause 'catastrophic injuries'.

Cheerleaders have a five-times higher chance of injury than less showy high-school girls, say North Carolina University orthopods. Their worst accidents are reported to the National Center for Catastrophic Sports Injury Research, which says cheerleading is behind more than half of all sport-related injuries resulting in death or hospitalization.

A study of 29 of the incidents recorded at the Center over a decade shows the easiest way to get severely hurt is to try building a human pyramid or performing a 'basket toss', where one cheerleader is thrown into the air. And if they are not the most popular girl in college, the rest of the team might just forget to catch them.

Catastrophic accidents include 17 severe head injuries, resulting in 13 skull fractures and two deaths; three damaged spinal cords, nine broken necks and major ligament injuries, say doctors in the *American Journal of Sports Medicine* (2003, 31; 6: 881). Go ambulance!

SCRUM STREP

Be careful who you head-butt, maul or grapple in manly contact sports. You could get a nasty infection.

Dr John Dorman, the student campus medic at America's Stanford University, discovered a new rugby-playing peril – what he calls scrum strep.

This is caused by a bacterial infection of the skin being passed from one player to another when they thud together. He tells in the *New England Journal of Medicine* (1981, 305; 8: 467) of a case in which a young man came to his clinic with a streptococcus infection of cuts on his thigh.

The lad went off to play in a local rugger tournament and, three days later, three more men showed up with the same streptococcus strain infecting their skin and throats. A few quick questions established that they had all been in the same scrum together. Similar outbreaks have occurred involving herpes in wrestlers in 1964, and among rugby players ten years later.

LIFEGUARD LUNG

So you fancy being a whistle-wielding Adonis in a singlet? Hold that thought. Not only do lifeguards have to enforce the local pool's 'no petting, no bombing, no running' rules, they also run the risk of contracting nasty lung infections.

Researchers studying outbreaks of lung disease at pools in Colorado, USA, discovered 33 lifeguards had lung damage due to infections. The longer the victims had worked as lifeguards, and the longer they worked each day at poolside, the greater their chance of illness.

The study, headed by C.S. Rose of the National Jewish Medical and Research Center, in Denver, found lifeguards faced up to five-times greater risk if they worked at a pool with a water-spray feature.

These sprays increase the quantity of toxic particles in the air by eight times, the study found. Improving the pools' ventilation systems didn't help, the scientists report in the *American Journal of Public Health* (1998, 88; 12: 1795). Preventing people urinating in the water might make a difference.

STRANGER THAN FRICTION

If the water spray doesn't get you, perhaps the slide will. Experts at Cincinnati University medical college's dermatology department report how they were asked to treat a 29-year-old man complaining of mysterious symmetrical patches on the back of both calves. The traumatized skin looked remarkably like alopecia.

The doctors questioned the man and found that he had spent the best part of a day playing on the water slides at a leisure park. Hence the big grazed areas on his legs.

Our superannuated water baby was not apparently smart enough to make the link himself – but at least he enabled the doctors to report the world's first case of water-slide alopecia in the skin journal, *Cutis* (2001, 67; 5: 399) along with a sage warning of the dangers of sports-related friction.

WATERSKIER'S ENEMA

Doctors at New York State University are worried about waterskiing. They say that if you are a woman waterskier and suffer a high-speed fall, you risk getting filled up with harmful torrents of liquid.

They say the problem occurs 'when a victim lands on the water at high speed with a cranio-rectal angle of about 120 degrees and the legs abducted' (that means lying back with your feet wide apart). Water is then forced at high pressure into any convenient female orifice.

That can cause hydrosalpinx – an accumulation of watery liquid in the fallopian tubes that is more normally associated with pelvic inflammatory disease. The doctors also say it can cause peritonitis – infection of the abdomen that can require hospitalization.

The team reports, in the *New England Journal of Medicine* (1980, 302; 22: 1264), that women's rectums also often get filled up with water. In patients suffering this, the doctors observed, 'sudden onset of crampy abdominal pain followed by intense desire to defecate'.

They add, 'defecation occurred in the immediate post-traumatic period and consisted of large amounts of blood-tinged fluid. All the victims recovered.'

They warn, however, 'The intense post-traumatic urge to defecate must be respected, and boat owners should carefully question anyone whom they suspect of having waterskier's enema before allowing them back in the boat.'

WATERSKIER SEER SYNDROME

It might seem rather fun to watch a waterskier self-enema in this manner. But watch out for waterskier seer syndrome, discovered by doctors at Massachusetts General Hospital. They say that people looking back out of the speedboat at the waterskier don't notice when their boat is about to hit a large wave or wake – so they get thrown over the side.

'The boat driver, as a reflex response, turns the boat away from the side of the fall, raising the stern of the boat and driving the propeller over the fallen passenger,' they tell the *New England Journal of Medicine* (1979, 300; 15: 865). 'In three cases, the patients sustained varying degrees of lacerating injuries to the face and upper extremities, which required emergency care and reconstructive surgery.'

SURFER'S EAR

More board-related havoc is caused by surfer's ear, which is not restricted to surfers. It can afflict anyone who spends time in cold water such as that found around the British Isles. It causes lesions in the ear canal, and can block it by up to 90 per cent. Understandably, sufferers complain that their ear feels blocked. Surgery is sometimes necessary, warns the journal *Otolaryngology Head and Neck Surgery* (2002, 126; 5: 499).

RUNNING INTO TROUBLE

Runners aren't immune from strange injuries either. Hazards include **penile frostbite** (*New England Journal of Medicine*, 1997, 296; 3: 178) – don't go running at night in winter, commando-style, while wearing thin shorts. And then there's **jogger's nipple** (bleeding nips caused by rubby clothes).

Swiss researchers warn joggers in *Schweiz Medizinische Wochenschrift* (1986, 116; 35: 1189) that 'collisions with vehicles and **injuries by buzzards** are further possible incidents to be reckoned with occasionally.' Now there's something you hadn't prepared for.

Then there is **runner's trot** – bloating, diarrhoea and flatulence experienced by long-distance runners bouncing their innards about, as revealed in the *Journal of the American Medical Association* (1980, 243; 17: 1743).

SHARON STONE SYNDROME

Don't try getting fit rapidly if you are over 40. You could end up like the star of the film, *Boxing Helena*. The *Independent* newspaper (26 November 2001) reports how doctors in California applied to the American Medical Association to register Sharon Stone syndrome in honour of the film star who, at the age of 43, was unfortunate enough to suffer a mild stroke the previous month while training for a three-mile charity run.

Researchers at Ohio State University claim there has been a massive increase in heart attacks and strokes among the YMAs (young middle-ageds). The scientists say that thousands of fortysomethings are being killed by exercise as they try to recapture the muscle tone of their youth.

SPOT-KICK KILLERS

Keep a defibrillator handy by the couch next time you watch international soccer. Heart attacks increased by a quarter when England lost to Argentina in a penalty shoot-out in the 1998 World Cup, say researchers at the Universities of Bristol and Birmingham in the *British Medical Journal* (2002, 325; 7378: 1439).

Risk of admission to hospital for heart attack increased by 25 per cent on 30 June 1998, the day of the shoot-out, and for the following two days. No increase in hospital admissions occurred on the previous England match days in that World Cup.

The researchers blame viewers' stress and conclude that, aside from questions of sporting fairness, the lottery of the penalty shoot-out should be abandoned on health grounds. Not least because England so often lose them.

INSTRUMENT INJURIES

Music can soothe the troubled soul, but it might not do much for your health if you are a classical player, according to a study of performers' music-related problems at a hand-surgery practice. The study of 167 patients aged from nine to 83 years found muscle-tendon strains were the most common problem, occurring principally among pianists, violinists, guitarists and reed instrumentalists.

The surgery discovered:

- *Pianists:* 55 per cent strains, 17 per cent inflammatory conditions, 13 per cent nerve problems
- *Violinists and viola players:* 64 per cent strains, 7 per cent inflammatory conditions
- *Guitarists:* 37.5 per cent strains, 22 per cent inflammatory conditions, 16 per cent nerve problems
- *Flautists:* 25 per cent strains, 45 per cent inflammatory conditions
- *Percussionists:* 36 per cent strains, 36 per cent inflammatory conditions

(Source: *Medical Problems of Performing Artists* (2002; 17: 135))

ART ATTACKS

Gospel concerts could take you closer to heaven than you expected. Your chances of needing medical help at a musical event depend on the type of music you listen to, says the journal, *Academic Emergency Medicine* (1999, 6; 3: 202).

* *Highest likelihood of medical emergency*: gospel
* *Lowest likelihood of medical emergency*: rhythm and blues
* *Highest likelihood of audience members having heart problems*: classical
* *Concert with the highest single-day record for medical emergencies*: grunge

Note of reality: the journal also points out that your chance of needing medical aid at any type of concert is about one in 30,000.

WHEN THE FAT LADY SINGS

Suicide expert Stephen Stack says opera fans have a heightened chance of topping themselves. The Wayne State University researcher argues in *Death Studies* (2002, 26; 5: 431) that they see so many performances where everyone on stage kills themselves at the end, that they are precisely 2.37 times more open to the idea of copying their example.

He calls this the **Madame Butterfly effect**, and looked to see if it also works in blues fans, who spend so much time listening to miserable music. He found no direct link, but concluded that listening to Blind Lemon Jefferson and Robert Johnson is more likely to make you reject religion. 'And low religiosity is the biggest risk factor for considering suicide,' he says.

IT TOLLS FOR THEE

Now surely you can't get much safer than bell ringing. However ... a review of six years' worth of that campanologists' must-read magazine, *Ringing World*, and a survey of 20 operational bell towers has revealed that a disturbing number of bell ringers end up getting tolled off. A total of 79 accidents resulted in ringers getting injured – and in some cases even killed, say doctors at Leicester Royal Infirmary in the *British Medical Journal* (1990, 301; 6766: 415).

LIVE LONG AND PROSPER

So just how do you cheat the Reaper?

The planet's longest-lived people are not necessarily the world's most healthy living ones. Mary Dorothy Christian, who was 113 years old and the United States' oldest person when she died in 2003, was a junk-food fiend. Kentucky Fried Chicken and Hostess Twinkies were among Christian's favourites right up until she died.

Sek Yi, a Cambodian tiger hunter said to be the world's oldest man when he died aged reportedly 122, attributed his longevity and that of his 108-year-old wife Long Ouk, to smoking and the power of prayer. 'When I was young I used to chew betel, but people made fun of me, saying I was like a woman, so I took up smoking,' he revealed.

The man confirmed by the *Guinness Book of Records* as the world's oldest ever, Shigechiyo Izumi of Japan, lived to be 120. His favourite drink was an alcoholic beverage called Shochu, which is distilled from barley.

So how do you stay alive, if it is not entirely about being medically healthy? The December 2003 issue of the *Mayo Clinic Women's Health Source* offers these tips:

- *Have a positive attitude.*
- *Eat well.*
- *Limit your alcohol consumption. Alcohol's effects are magnified with age.*

- *Stop smoking.*
- *Stay physically active.*
- *Reduce stress by controlling how you react to stressful situations.*
- *Keep your brain in shape. Lifelong learning is important.*
- *Keep your social bonds strong. Having a dependable group of friends and family is one of the most reliable predictors of longevity.*
- *Nurture your spirituality.*
- *Plan your finances for the future.*

Or there's the moral view. From 1921 until 1995, Lewis Terman followed the lives of 1,528 children in California who had been marked out for having high IQs.

By 1995, half of them were dead. But the study in *Science* (1995, 267: 1269) concluded that bright children, especially boys, will live longer if they are prudent, conscientious, truthful and free from vanity.

So now you know. Probably. Possibly. Maybe. Perhaps.

INDEX